LIVING THE FAITH COMMUNITY

LIVING THE FAITH COMMUNITY

The Church
That Makes a Difference

John H. Westerhoff, III

WINSTON PRESS

Library of Congress Catalog Card Number: 84-52502

ISBN: 0-86683-870-8

Printed in the United States of America

5   4   3   2   1

Winston Press, Inc.
430 Oak Grove
Minneapolis, Minnesota 55403

For

*my mother, Nona; my father, John Jr.; my brother,
Jeff; my mother-in-law, Elizabeth; my father-in-law,
Albert; my sister-in-law, Florence; my wife, Barnie;
our children, Jill, Jack, and Beth; our godchild,
Kristen; and the congregations of many traditions—
Presbyterian, Reformed Church in America,
Evangelical United Brethren, United Methodist,
United Church of Christ, Roman Catholic, and
Episcopal—of which this family has been a part for
over fifty years*

Contents

1

The Church as Family

The family and family life have changed and are changing. Most of us have experienced some of the resulting disease, but few of us know the cure. Those of us who are Christians know instinctively that the church holds the clues to the cure; but in our experience the church, at best, has addressed only symptoms while the disease remains.

With the birth of a child, parents raised in the church typically think first of baptism. For some, the reason may be fear: Baptism is a magical act to convince God to do something for our child, something that God would not do unless we performed the correct ritual. For others, the reason may be custom: Baptism is an act expected of decent parents. For still others, the reason may be the desire to share with their children life in the body of Christ. Still, in spite of our various reasons, all seem to sense unconsciously that they can't go it alone. If their children are to have Christian faith and live the Christian life, they will need to be nurtured in that faith and life. And that cannot be done adequately outside a community of faith.

While the family will always be a primary context for nurture, the modern family's authority is limited; a complex configuration of societal forces impinge upon its influence. In the nineteenth century, when Horace Bushnell wrote *Christian Nurture*, it was important to stress nurture within the family. But we cannot frame a contemporary theory of Christian nurture based upon an image of the family or of the church from another era in history. Because we face unique problems in our day, new understandings must emerge.

Throughout church history, both singleness and marriage have been considered Christian vocations. While in some periods one or the other was thought more holy, the church has maintained that both are proper contexts in which to do the will of God and witness to the gospel. Unfortunately, in our own day many persons have assumed that only marriage can lead to meaningful life.

As a result, some who should remain single get married and destroy the relationship. Others feel inadequate and unfulfilled because they never have the opportunity to be married. Some feel guilty because they do not wish to be married. Still others have connected singleness to priesthood or the "religious life" and therefore have denied ordination to persons who also choose marriage.

But life, whether single or married, requires community. Therefore, it is the church—a faith community—not the cultural family, which is essential to Christian faith and life. The foundation of Christian life is life in the church.

Jesus consistently denied primary obligations to his cultural family and committed himself unreservedly to his "faith family." The clearest statement we have about Jesus' attitude toward family relations is a passage from Mark's account of the gospel (3:7-35). Surrounded by his followers, hounded by critics, and now pursued by his frightened mother and distraught family members, Jesus answered the question, "Who are my mother and brothers?" by saying, "They are those who do the will of God!"

Jesus announced that from that point onward kinship would no longer be defined biologically. Jesus claimed as members of his family those who shared his vision and acted accordingly. The members of his own cultural family were not excluded from this new fellowship, but neither were they automatically included.

In Matthew's account of the gospel, Jesus is even more radical. Here he speaks of dividing cultural families in the name of a faith family (10:34-37). Nevertheless, Jesus never condemns the family as an institution or suggests that living in a cultural family is not part of God's intention for humankind. He simply puts the faith family first and suggests that those who relinquish traditional family ties will gain a new and ultimately more important family to nurture and sustain them in faith.

The first great crisis in the life of the Christian church was related to biological kinship. Paul made it his life's work to convince Jewish Christians that the inheritance of God's promise to Abraham came not through blood lines but through radical faith in the death and resurrection of Jesus. The future of the church depended on altering—that is, broadening and expanding—the notion of kinship and covenant relationships. While showing deep concern for the cultural family by acts such as baptizing whole households, the church understood itself as an expression of *the family of God* and asked for a familial commitment from its members.

Those who embraced the gospel were members of cultural families, but Jesus called them out of their families and into a new family—a family not identified by genealogy or even clan association but by the covenanting of God with them. This new family was regarded as the household of God and, according to its self-understanding, was the family through whom all other families would be blessed. For Jesus and the early church the Christian community offered a new kind of family, gathered together and united in a common faith and life, a community between the natural family and society and, on occasion, a community in tension with both.

Before exploring how the revolutionary character of the gospel transformed the notion of the family, it is important to examine the history of the cultural family. Through much of history and in most cultures, human beings have not lived in a nuclear or even an extended family. Rather they have lived in social units best described as clans or tribes. Tribal families or clans—groups of persons and assorted kin forming a close residential community for the mutual benefit of its members—are a basic unit of human life.

While nuclear family units can be found in the ancient world, the tribe was the basic social unit. In the world of biblical history, the tribe was the basic unit of meaning that shaped and defined reality. When the Old Testament speaks of a family, it is referring to a tribal family that (being patriarchal) included a husband, his wives and their children, his concubines and their children, sons and daughters-in-law and their offspring, slaves of both sexes and their children, dependents such as the parentless, widows, and illegitimate children, aliens such as the sojourner passing through, and all the marginal folk who choose to live among the group.

However, as human life became more complex, the tribal family necessarily and wisely split into a primary unit of life known as the extended family and a number of secondary social institutions. But the term "extended family" is misleading because the name implies that the nuclear family is normative and that the extended family is composed of numerous nuclear families. In reality, the nuclear family is a *restricted* family, a late adaption of the extended family, which itself was an adaption of the tribal family.

This so-called extended family was comprised of

three or more generations living together and interacting for one another's mutual benefit—essentially a kinship group living in a common household or in close geographical proximity. Society assumed responsibility for those who did not live in these extended families and for facilitating harmony among the various family units.

A functional analysis of the tribal family reveals five significant functions:

1. Reproduction—It provided the means for the tribe to replace its dying members and perpetuate itself;
2. Nurture—It provided the means to sustain and transmit the tribe's shared understandings and ways of life, as well as those skills necessary for survival;
3. Security—It provided the means to protect tribal members from disaster, external attack, illness, and feebleness;
4. Physical survival—It provided the basic means of production and a necessary division of labor to meet needs such as housing, clothing, and food;
5. Support—It provided the means to meet various human psychological needs, such as intimacy.

Later, most of these functions were at least partially adopted by the extended family. But with an increasingly industrial economy and an emerging urban, mobile society, the nuclear family emerged and passed on an increasing number of these functions to the state or other social institutions.

Today these secondary institutions have assumed significant aspects of all the family's societal functions, save procreation. (From a biological point of view, the society can now take over this function.) Nurture is increasingly conducted in nurseries, in day-care centers, in schools, and through the mass media. Security is provided by insurance companies, retirement centers, fire and police departments, and hospitals. The provision of food, clothing, and shelter, and the division of labor necessary for this provision have been assumed by business and industry. Support, while still centered in the family, is increasingly supplied by clubs, voluntary associations, professional therapists, and counselors.

The contemporary cultural family is slowly being dispossessed of all its functions; even procreation is considered optional rather than essential for group survival. The place of the family and expectations of the family have radically changed during this generation. In no previous period of history has the social order been organized as it is now or functioned the way it now does. We are the first people to try to live and maintain life within the particular societal structures we have created.

The family is a configuration, culturally and historically influenced, of which there are countless variants. Throughout history the cultural family has adapted to changing social realities, but not in any evolutionary progression. In America, for example, up through the eighteenth century the family was understood as a little church and commonwealth that closely shared the wider society's understanding and ways of life. Then early in the nineteenth century the family became a separate entity, defining itself in part over and against the society. The new family became the family of refuge, a bastion of repose, orderliness, and unwavering devotion of persons to each other. With a sharp delineation of roles and responsibilities, husbands worked in one world according to one set of values, and women and children lived in another world safe from the pressures, temptations, and evils of the world outside. To this homeland the man of the family would retreat for refreshment and renewal. So it was that the eighteenth century Puritan family of social integration gave way to the nineteenth century Victorian family of escape. The twentieth century marks one more radical shift in the history of the family.

Today we witness a continuing transformation of the family. The changes involved are not in themselves either good or evil; but like all other social realities they can be either or both. Surely the Christian family cannot be identified with any particular social pattern. As believers in Christ and members of his church, Christians can choose to live within various family relationships: extended families, nuclear families, single-parent families, and families without children, to name just a few.

From an historical perspective, the family has always been changing. Knowing this, we gain nothing by constructing in our imaginations the "perfect family" or a "Christian family." What many people call the "normal family"—a mother, father, and their children living in a single household, with the mother working at home and assuming primary responsibility for child-rearing—is not necessarily the healthiest or best model for family life.

Many different styles of healthy family relationships are possible among Christians. Who comprises a family, how the family is structured, what roles each member plays, how long children live at home with their parents, how much attention fathers pay to infants, what work mothers perform outside the home, whether it is God's will to bear children, and whether one is called to marriage or singleness: All these issues have various Christian answers.

Surely the Christian family cannot be identified with any particular pattern. Whether or not it is Christian depends upon the faith of its members and the character of the life it shares, not upon its structures, the roles persons play within it, or the functions it performs. It is irrational to conclude, as some have done, that the ideal Christian family is the nuclear family with roles defined by sex.

The cultural family is not dying, nor is the nuclear family outmoded. The family, in its various manifestations, continues to play a crucial role in the social order. It continues to influence significantly the lives of its members.

But the family *has* changed. It is now a dependent social unit of consumption, rather than an independent unit of production. The state increasingly has assumed the functions of nurture traditionally reserved for the family. Persons live longer, more chose singleness, the family unit becomes smaller as more chose not to have children, and the generations live independent of each other. The family has become more dependent upon society's political, social, and economic institutions and less dependent upon its own members. Marriages are increasingly comprised of equal partners living in both independent and mutually satisfying relationships. The decision to live together outside the covenant of marriage, in both homosexual and heterosexual relationships, increases, as does divorce. Whether these trends continue or are reversed, some form of the cultural family will exist and play a significant role in the lives of many people.

At the same time, the political, social, and economic institutions of government are changing radically as well. Larger and more impersonal, they are increasingly competitive, specialized, bureaucratic, and out of touch with the people. Created to serve humanizing forces within society, they tend to evolve into alienating structures with dehumanizing programs.

Some governmental leaders today advocate that this trend be reversed. As appealing as that perspective may sound, it is clear that we cannot return all responsibility for human life to the private sector. Governmental services are essential to modern life, and they can—indeed must—contribute significantly to justice and humane life. But they cannot replace other social units or satisfactorily assume all the functional responsibilities of the family.

The responses to this contemporary family situation are varied. Some long to return to the past by recreating the traditional (somewhat imaginary) cultural family; but we can't go home again. Some strive to recreate the tribal family by constructing communes; but unless we are to reverse history, communal life is not an option for North American society in general.

Despite these realities, the typical family, though perhaps well-suited to the mobility of the contemporary era, can never be a fully adequate social unit for human life. Nor can the social, political, and economic institutions we have created to support the family and address human needs. Attempts to reform and humanize both the family and the state and its related institutions, while important and necessary, can never be adequate or sufficient. For neither family nor government nor the two together can satisfactorily address the human problems and needs of our modern communications society. A third alternative is needed.

That alternative is for the church to become a *mid-community*, that is, a faith community that exists between the family on one side and the society and its institutions on the other. In other words, I am recommending that the church become for Christians the most central, foundational unit of societal life.

The issue for the church, therefore, is not, how we can humanize or help the family and the state to be more humane and effective, but how we can reform the church so that it can become a faith community for the humanization of all persons and social life.

The first difficulty with this concept is that we often do not think of the church as a faith community. For most people, the church is one voluntary association alongside others, one of the many clubs or societal institutions to which they choose to belong. Further, we commonly think of Christian life from an individualistic or, at best, an organizational perspective, but rarely from a communal perspective.

The essential nature of religious community is hard to grasp here on a continent where evangelists typically strive to win souls for Christ, but rarely for Christ and his church; where baptism is understood as a call to individual salvation, rather than an incorporation into a family; where the Eucharist is seen as food for the individual soul rather than a communal thanksgiving meal; and where the church is believed to be a voluntary association to which we individually belong by choice and withdraw at will, rather than an eternal relationship established by God, binding us together to be a sign and witness of God's reign in human history.

Church is expressed uniquely in families. The nuclear family remains a basic unit of society and religion. As *Lumen Gentium* put it, "The family is the domestic church." The family is not like the church, nor just a part of the church; the family is the church in miniature, for it has within it everything essential.

In *Family Ministry*, Marie and Brennan Hill note that the family expresses the presence of Christ, that is, the spirit of unconditional forgiving love and compassion; it represents the experience of fellowship with Christ, that is, diverse personalities, ages, and sexes living in harmony; and it manifests life in Christ, that is, self-sacrificing, caring, and seeking the good of others.

Now while the family is indeed a little church, the family cannot *be* the church. The family may give an image of what the church is called to be, but the family cannot be the church unless it is united with other families in a community of faith. Too often we read that the family should do better at being the church; but the family is too small, too fragmented, too isolated to be the church. To force one more responsibility on this fragile unit of human life is to destroy it. If the church really cared about family life, it would be a community in which families could share responsibilities, reduce pressures, and give one another support in their relationship to God, self, neighbor, and the natural world.

The difficulty, however, is finding such a community of faith. The issue seems clear: Is the church willing to reform its life so that congregations can become communities of faith or faith families, and thereby provide a home for the various cultural families and households in which persons live?

Christian parents are called to bring up their children in the church. They are to share *with* their children in the journey of faith within a community of faith. The church must stop doing things *to* families by burdening them with the complete responsibility of nurturing their children in the Christian faith. The church must also stop doing things *for* families by assuming all responsibility for nurturing children in the faith.

The church, as a community of faith, must begin to do things *with* families and single persons. The best ministry the church can provide for or to cultural families and single persons is to be a community for all people, no matter what their social arrangement—separated, widowed, childless, divorced, single parent, nuclear family, extended family, even the single person who lives alone or in a "family" made up of roommates or friends.

The implications should be obvious. Single persons and cultural families need the church. We all need the church. Without life in community we cannot acquire, sustain, or deepen Christian faith and life. But the church as we know it may need to be reformed, and we may need to change radically our understandings and ways of life. Community comes at a price—a price we may not want to pay.

2

The Christian's Need for Community

Jesus said, "Where two or three are gathered together in my name, there I am in the midst of them" (Matthew 18:19-20). It is this mystery of gathering together in a particular way that the word "church" is intended to express.

As Christ is the sacrament of God, the church is the sacrament of Christ. The church is the body of Christ, a union in love, a oneness in Spirit, a life in common. It is an outward and visible manifestation of an inward and spiritual reality known as grace, that communal relationship that God has with us and we are to have with one another.

God is described best in terms of the holy and blessed Trinity, for God is experienced as one who lives in community and expresses self as community—three distinct persons in one, acting together throughout all time as Creator, Redeemer, and Perfecter of the world and all that is in it. And we who are in the image of God are intended to live in community: a relationship of *creativity* with God, cultivating, preserving, and humanizing the natural world; a relationship of *reconciliation* with one another, expressing the redemption of the world through justice and peace; and a relationship of *friendship* with God, fullness of life in an ever deepening and loving intimacy.

St. John Chrysostom commented in his homily on Ephesians, "St. Paul demands such love of us, a love which should bind us one to the other so that we no more should be separated one from the other; . . . St. Paul demands that our union should be as perfect as is that of the members of one body."

The Christian commandment to love means that we are to love all others as ourselves, to see our own selves in others, indeed in all others. As we do this, we are enabled both to see ourselves and our vulnerability in the most broken, distorted of human beings and to see Christ in them so that we can also see Christ in ourselves. 'Xst in you" — hope I glory etc .

One of Henri Nouwen's students once noted to him, "Whenever I'm with you, it is as if I am in the presence of Christ." It is said that Father Nouwen responded, "It is the Christ in you who sees the Christ in me." Similarly, the story is told that one cold night a woman who was in the last stages of syphilis was invited by Dorothy Day to share her bed. Dorothy is quoted as saying to her friend Catherine Doherty, "I don't see a woman with syphilis; I only see the image of Christ."

Upon hearing those anecdotes one of my students commented, "Isn't all that a bit idealistic and romantic? It may be good theology, but it is terribly out of step with reality and human experience. If theology is supposed to make sense out of life, you have just failed." Another student broke in, "But don't we wish it were true?"

Community is a great ideal. Everybody wants it; few achieve it. And the church rarely offers it. Yet people still search for it.

Sociologist Robert Nisbet, in his book *The Quest For Community*, documents our loss of community. He challenges modernity's emphasis on the individual at the expense of the relationships and communal symbols necessary for human life. The contemporary stress upon the autonomous individual, he says, has led to estrangement and isolation of persons from each other, the shattering of the human-divine relationship, and atomization of the personality. As a result, persons increasingly are seeking community and relational life. Nisbet states that this quest for community will not be denied, because it springs from the very nature of human life.

Because of his strong theological conviction that life was fundamentally social, Horace Bushnell in his seminal work *Christian Nurture* sought to provide an alternative to individualism and privatised religious experience. He argued for Christian nurture within the family and a family-like church because he believed that human life was dependent upon relationships. To this nineteenth century New England divine, surrounded by the enthusiasm of American individualistic frontier pietism, Christian faith and life depended upon —indeed, could not be separated from—Christian community.

"One Christian is no Christian (that's Pascal)," I recently wrote in a journal essay. "There can be no health, no wholeness and holiness, outside of community." A number of the journal reviewers objected that my position was too strong. "Would the anchorites who lived alone in caves during early centuries of the church disagree?" queried the editor. He did not seem to understand that while the anchorites were in solitude and silence, they were not alone or outside of communication. In those solitary caves they were surrounded by angels, archangels, and all the company of heaven, and they were in communication and community with the God, the holy and blessed Trinity, who also lives in community.

Anthropologist Colin Turnbull, a student of Pygmy life, contends that the study of simple societies can aid in the understanding of human life in complex societies. He argues that contemporary North American culture is dehumanizing because it lacks the elements necessary to bind individuals into community. We worship individual wealth and idealize the self-made person. We aspire to materialistic and isolated goals for life, so we become increasingly possessive and estranged from one another. We may proclaim equality, cooperation, and community, but we teach inequality, competition, and individualism.

When people were fixing up People's Park in Berkeley, California, some took shovels and began digging a hole. No one really talked about why they were digging the hole, but every day they continued. Others would also stop and dig for a while, and soon the hole got deeper and deeper. The participants did not recognize any sort of leadership or community life. At first, they thought they would make a fountain, but the hole was getting too big. So they considered a wading pool for kids, but the hole was getting too big. Others recommended a swimming pool and just kept digging.

One day someone started shoveling the dirt back into the hole. "Hey, what do you think you are doing?" someone who was shoveling the dirt out shouted angrily. "You feel like shoveling dirt out," the response came. "I feel like shoveling dirt in. I'm doing my thing, just like you are doing yours."

In our sports and secular rituals we honor inequality by encouraging activities in which players theoretically begin as equals and end up as unequals. There are always winners and losers; a tie is considered unsatisfactory to everyone.

Even our language suggests violence and individuality. "I'm going to beat you," we say. We know full well that our success will be at the expense of others. We honor cooperation but in a socially destructive way. That is, we encourage absolute cooperation with the

-16-

members of our team in order to "beat hell" out of the other team. In this hostile act is the seed of nationalism and international conflict. We honor individualism to such a point that at the Super Bowl, our most communal national ritual, we insist on rewarding a "Most Valuable" player.

Turnbull contends that we lack rituals that will bring us closer to one another and that we both worship individual success and believe that independence and freedom are the ultimate values. But can we be fully human in such a world? Most of us would, in the end, answer no. We long for and search for community, and when a crisis comes, we act in communal ways. We know we need community, but in our culture it keeps eluding us.

Over a decade ago in *The Pursuit of Loneliness* Philip Slater explored three human drives and their frustrations in our culture. The first is the desire for *community*, the wish to live in trust and cooperation with others as brothers and sisters. This desire is frustrated by culture's stress upon individualism and competition to the point that collectivism is all but unknown to us and cooperation, while present, is peripheral to our experience.

The second drive is the desire for *engagement*, our wish to solve social and interpersonal problems cooperatively. This desire is frustrated by our loss of hope in being able to solve social problems or even to influence change. While we continue to respond personally to the needs of others, we become increasingly uninvolved in social issues.

The third human drive is the desire for *dependence*, our wish to share responsibility for life and that of others. This desire is frustrated by the value we put on independence and the resultant autonomous pursuit of our own personal destiny. We have become so enculturated, Slater contended, that when our natural human drive for community surfaces, we still remain wary of group demands, resent group restraints, and are suspicious of group problem solving and decision making.

As Evelyn and James Whitehead point out in *Community of Faith*, we are ambivalent about community. On the one hand we desire communal life, and on the other hand we are committed to individualism. We want to share life and work, to be bound together by trust and compassion, but we remain committed to the autonomous pursuit of our own destiny and the rightful possession of what we have earned. We want the support that comes from belonging to a community of shared values, and yet we resent group restraints and binding ethical principles.

We want a community that will make us feel at home in a bureaucratic world, but we are wary of group demands and expectations. We want the benefits of community without any of its responsibilities. We want the church to replace the ethnic-religious neighborhood and the extended family, but we want that done without any of the limits on individuals inherent in those social structures.

We want community, but we do not want what community requires. We may not like or find meaningful and satisfying our modern, impersonal, bureaucratic, competitive, individualistic, privatized society; but we are unwilling to give up what we count as its benefits in order to have a personal, familial, cooperative, communal, public society.

We acknowledge the dehumanizing character of modernity, but we have become so enculturated that we seem unable to free ourselves from its ways in order to find a more humane way to live. We really don't want the obligations of communal authority; we prefer to have individual authority. We really don't want the obligations of communal worship; we prefer to pray when, where, and how we desire. We really don't want the obligations of a communal memory and vision; we prefer to tell our own stories, and live for our own aims. We really don't want the obligations of communal life; we prefer to live autonomously. We really don't want to obey the authority of ethical norms; we prefer a situational, privatistic ethic.

Of course, all this may be, in part, the consequence of living in a male-dominated society and church. Carol Gilligan, the Harvard psychologist who wrote *In a Different Voice*, discovered in her research that men and women have different ways of speaking about moral problems and of describing themselves and their relationships with others. Men tend to think of themselves in terms of self-identity, to value freedom, and to judge life by the standards of rights and personal achievements. Women tend to think of themselves in terms of relationships with others or intimacy, to value equality, and to judge life by the standard of responsibility and care. Interestingly, she discovered that the literature on human development interpreted the failure of women to fit existing models of human growth based on male norms as a problem in women's development, rather than a limitation in our understanding of the human condition and maturity.

Similarly, in *Women's Reality* Anne Wilson Schaef points out that for men the center of the universe is the self and work. Indeed, while everything is defined in terms of the self, relationships and human interactions are hierarchical: One person is superior and the other inferior. Intimacy is considered a physical act of individuals, and commitment is seen as a loss of freedom.

In contrast, for women the center of the universe is relationships and people. Relationships are understood as associations of equals. Intimacy is considered the mutual sharing of total beings, and commitment is seen as a covenantal relationship. While Schaef does not say so, women's perspective seems more consistent with Christian values, faith, and life than its alternative.

-19-

So the feminine concern for relationships and communal life is important for the church.

After having read the books of Gilligan and Schaef, one of my students shared how for two years she has served on the admissions committee at the seminary, reading applications from prospective students. She had observed a difference between the descriptions given by men and women about their sense of "call" to ministry but could not understand it. Suddenly, she said, it was clear. The men understood their call as an autonomous, dramatic separating out; the women as a relational, slow coming to awareness. To male readers, the women appeared unclear, less than sure, and indecisive.

Susan Brooks Thistlethwaite's book, *Metaphors for the Contemporary Church*, is a provocative attempt to probe the relationship between metaphors for the church and the status of women within the church. Her thesis is that in those times when the church emphasizes qualities typically associated with women—cooperation, integration, and affiliation—women are well represented and accepted in the church. Conversely, when values stereotypically connected with men—competition, individualism, hierarchical relations, and aggressiveness—are ascendant, women will be excluded. She further examines the principal metaphors Christians have used throughout history to depict those experiences of the church. Of these, she sees "the body of Christ" and "the family of God" (feminine images) as essential to the revitalization of the modern church.

In an address to the bishops of the Episcopal Church in the United States on the theme of ministry in an apocalyptic time, the Canadian Anglican priest Herbert O'Driscoll asserted that if the church were to survive and meet the needs of people in our time, it would need to change from a predominantly "masculine" goal- and task-oriented religious institution to a more "feminine" (not female or effeminate) nurturing and caring faith community. ⅄

While the call to a common life has been constant, the forms this community has assumed are varied. Parker Palmer, in his book *The Community of Strangers*, contends that Christian community forms in reaction to life in the larger society. For example, the early church became a disciplined, committed cadre for support in an alien world. After the church was socially sanctioned, it became synonymous with the body politic. Partly in order to preserve an endangered tradition, monasticism developed.

Today we experience a disconnected, disintegrated, depersonalized society of autonomous individuals living competitively within a violent, estranged world. We, therefore, image the church as an intimate, closely-knit, and homogeneous familial community in retreat from the world and public life. Palmer points out that such an idealized image is unrealizable. Moreover, it encourages escapist behavior and thereby denies the gospel's call to heterogeneity and the transforming of culture.

God's reign comes when we can regard all strangers as sisters and brothers; when we can embrace those from whom we are estranged; when we can unite in one congregation diverse racial, social, political, economic, and ethnic groups; when we can seek justice for those who are least deserving or lovable; when we are freed from private life, private property, and private commitment and led into public life, public property, and public commitment; and when the needs and concerns of the world's outcasts are made our agenda for prayers and service. Christian community is that place where the persons we least want to associate with and those least deserving have a rightful claim on all that we have and are.

Christian community is a style of life. The local church or parish should never strive to be as small as a primary group that encourages face-to-face interaction among all its members on a regular basis, that maintains high levels of emotional sharing and support, and that seeks to establish homogeneity and compatibility among all its members. While groups of this nature may exist profitably for short periods of time within the church, they can never become the church. Neither should the local church be so large that persons do not know each other, are unaware of one another's needs, interact only irregularly, make formal contact only on committees or task forces, and are so diverse that they hold nothing in common save their membership in the group.

A pitfall of small communities is that they can be closed. Often their life creates warm feelings of the nearness of God, but they can remain untouched by any impulse to share God's love. A kind of "coziness" can develop that shuts out those who did not belong to the community when it first formed. New persons can have difficulty feeling accepted; their possible influence can be neglected.

A Christian community is most functional and effective when it includes between 200 and 400 persons representing at least three generations, and a diversity of racial, ethnic, political, and economic groups. Such a community is small enough for human interaction and caring but not so small as to be incestuous and too homogeneous. The church needs to share a common identity and yet be open to others. It cannot be so open that it lacks a distinctive character or so distinctive in its identity that it is closed to others. The community we search for must be true community—somewhere between a primary group or family of kin and a formal association or societal institution.

In his classic *Faith and Nurture*, H. Shelton Smith wrote in 1941 that the fundamental issue for Christian nurture was ecclesiology, the nature of the church or Christian community. I agree, as do many others, and suspect that in the next few years we will see a number of books on the church and Christian education.

Ever since I wrote *Values For Tomorrow's Children* in 1972, I have emphasized the essential importance of the context in which catechesis or Christian nurture takes place. I have alluded to the characteristics needed in a faith community if Christian faith is to be acquired and enlivened, if divine revelation is to be made known, and if our Christian vocation is to be realized. There are other important issues related to catechesis or Christian nurture, but these fundamental questions about the nature of Christian community need to be resolved before the others become relevant or useful.

Charles Foster, writing in Seymour and Miller's book *Contemporary Approaches to Christian Education*, describes a faith-community model of Christian education and correctly describes my theoretical and practical work on Christian education as being guided by this image. While affirming this model's value, he warns that such faith communities simply do not and are not likely to exist in the near future. Therefore, he questions whether it is reasonable—in a society governed by assumptions and expectations of volunteerism, individualism, and privatism—to build a theory of Christian education on an image of a community of faith.

While I am aware of this serious limitation, I am convinced that until we have manifested the characteristics of a faith community, all our efforts at Christian nurture will be less than effective. So also are the authors of two of the most original and stimulating books on Christian education to appear in recent times: Australian Denham Grierson, who addresses the nature of Christian community and what shapes and sustains it in

Transforming a People of God, and Wim Saris SDB, a Dutch Roman Catholic religious educator, writing in his *Towards a Living Church.*

As H. Shelton Smith explains in *Faith and Nurture,* Christian nurture presupposes a medium, the church. Nevertheless, religious educators have tended to be unconcerned about the nature of Christian community and to minimize the communal nature of Christian faith and life. Instead they have focused upon individual religious experiences, beliefs, and behaviors and understood the church as a voluntary association of committed individuals uniting for institutional purposes. Smith asserts that persons are communal beings who in order to be Christian need to participate in churches that are communities of faith; without faithful communal life there can be no Christian faith or life.

I agree that a communal understanding of the church is necessary to meet the human need for communal life and restore the vision—central to the New Testament—of the church as the body of Christ and the people of God. Other contemporary theologians have written on the same theme. Karl Rahner contends that there has to be a church in a Christian understanding of faith and human existence, for Christianity comes to persons not through ideology or a religious experience but through life in a historical community. Emil Brunner argued that the church is not so much an institution as a community of persons. Dietrich Bonhoeffer developed the notion of the church as an interpersonal community. Yves Congar maintained that the church is fundamentally a community.

In *Models of the Church,* Avery Dulles identifies and describes five models for Christian community: the institutional, the mystical communion, the sacramental, the herald, and the servant models. The institutional model focuses its life on authority and communal norms, the mystical communion on shared common life of a familial nature, the sacramental on cultic (liturgical) life which makes Christ present, the herald on remembering and re-presenting a sacred narrative, and the servant on mission and ministry in the world. He contends that a proper understanding of the church integrates all these models. It is interesting to note that at various times in history one or another of these models has dominated. Similarly, different denominations have advocated one or another so as to remind other Christians of that model's importance.

For a number of years I have described the four necessary characteristics of a Christian faith community as (1) a common story or memory and vision, (2) a common authority, (3) common rituals, and (4) a common life together that is more like a family than an institution. The correspondence to Dulles' models should be obvious; it is also intentional. While Christian community cannot be built, it has particular signs that are also preconditions of its presence as a gift.

This book is about those signs and preconditions of Christian community. Persons long for such community; indeed, it is necessary for fully human life and for Christian witness in the modern world. In the following chapters we will explore (1) the narrative character of Christian community, (2) the role of worship as an authority for Christian life, (3) the liturgical experience necessary for Christian transformation and formation, and (4) the common life in Christ that nurtures an alternative consciousness among those who live in the world but not of the world.

3

The Narrative Character
of Christian Community

Richard Adams' novel *Watership Down* illustrates the significance of a common memory and vision for communal life. In his insightful adventure story, the characters (rabbits, in this case) become a people only as they acquire a story: a memory and a vision. They remain a community only insofar as they retell the story and live for the vision. Adams' depiction of various communities suggests that each is made viable by its ability to sustain a narrative.

Christians, likewise, are a story-formed community, a people on a journey. The Christian church was founded upon a story of a people's experiences with Jesus and a vision of God's reign in human history. Throughout the church's history this story has formed and transformed, sustained and challenged the community's faith and life.

In Peter Shaffer's play *Equus* an adolescent boy has blinded a number of horses after being seduced by a woman employee of the stable. His psychiatrist's task is to analyze the cause of the young man's psychotic behavior and free him for productive life. What is unveiled in the drama is the mental torment of a patient and the story he develops in an attempt to make that torment tolerable. It soon becomes evident that if the boy is to endure the vicissitudes of life, a story will be necessary.

"We need a story to see in the dark," the psychiatrist comments.

We all need a story. Stories are reality. Stories provide us with both a memory linking us meaningfully to the past and a vision calling us to a purposeful future. That memory and that vision make life in the present possible. Without a story we would live in an unreal world, life would make no sense. Without a story we could not live, we could not have community. The story that is foundational to our life provides us with the basis for our perceptions or faith, as well as for our character and moral life. The story that forms Christian community is comprised of a common memory and a common vision.

A common memory: It is essential that we share a common sacred story to explain the meaning and purpose of life and that we transmit it to the next generation. Unless this shared story is alive and shared, the gift of community will elude us.

Jews (in contrast to Christians) put five commandments on each of the two tablets representing the Ten Commandments. One side lists those concerning humankind's relationship with God and the other side those regarding relationships with human neighbors. The one commandment that Jews put on the "God side" and we Christians put on the "neighbor side" is, "Honor your father and mother" (Exodus 20:12). Christians commonly interpret this commandment solely in terms of human relationships. Jews understand it as indicating that honor, deference, and respect should be given to all the elderly, because they have the memory of who we are; without their memory we cannot know or relate to the God who is God, who loves us and saves us.

A common vision: We need to share not only an understanding of the past but also a desired and anticipated

we need to have a belief of meaning re: justice

future. We need visions, and wherever a vision is shared, the gift of community is made possible.

Harmon Smith, an Episcopal priest, tells of visiting Dachau, Germany, and becoming sick from the experience of seeing what Christians did to Jews. Reflecting on the Holocaust with Pastor Reiger, a member of the Lutheran Confessing Church and one who himself had been a prisoner at Dachau, Smith asked, "How could this have happened in the land of Luther and Bach?"

"That is easy to understand," the old man responded. "The Christian church had become concerned with the here and now, a very practical institution; it had lost its visions and forgotten what the Bible teaches—'without a vision the people perish.' But," he continued, "Hitler remembered, and he gave our people a vision."

Christians are a people on a pilgrimage through seasons of profane time made holy by the eternal cycle of sacred time. The church needs to find a way to live God's re-creative story so that it touches, illumines, transforms, and forms personal and corporate lives to serve God's purposes day by day.

My book *A Pilgrim People* makes the radical suggestion that we let the church year provide the basis for the church's life and program. By so doing we would not only celebrate the Christian story but experience and live it through our participation in the life of the church. Life in a story-formed community would then have the possibility of forming our personal lives so that individually and corporately we might manifest that story for all the world to see; thus we would be a sign and witness to God's action in history on behalf of all people.

While the church's story is contained in the Holy Scripture and summarized in the Apostles' and Nicene Creeds, it is presented in the church year in a unique way. Of course, one way to look at the church year is in terms of doctrine (both Scripture and revelation can be

Pl. see

treated as doctrine or as event). For example, Christmas focuses on incarnation, Easter on redemption, and so forth. Another way is to look at the church year in terms of historical events. The church year in this case begins with Advent and goes through Pentecost. For example, Christmas celebrates Jesus' birthday, and Easter his resurrection.

A third way is to look at the church year as story: the story of God's action in history and the story of the church's continuing struggle to make sense of God's story and to live it. Christians in every age attempt to integrate the church's story with their own stories, so *p. life* that the community's story can become their own. When we envision the church year as story, we remember and retell the story in ways that continually shape and reshape our lives in community.

From this perspective, the church year ends on Wednesday of Holy Week with the celebration of Tenebrae and begins on Thursday of Holy Week with the Maundy Thursday celebration of foot washing and Eucharist, the beginning of the Paschal feast and the Easter cycle. The Paschal mystery, the Easter story, is *the* story that forms and re-forms the church; this is why every Sunday is a little Easter.

Easter, the story of a new beginning for all human life and social history, celebrates the victory of God, the triumph of good over evil. It signals the reign of life over death through the liberating, suffering, reconciling, redeeming, transforming love of God. Through the comic drama of salvation God has revealed to the world that every human being is created in God's image. And to what end? For life in relationship to God and to other persons in a world under God's benevolent, compassionate rule of justice and peace. Indeed, each Sunday in the Eucharist we celebrate this holy mystery of a new beginning.

Eastertide, a time of new beginnings, is the honey-moon season of the church year—a time when we live in defiance of what appears to be reality and live for the true reality of the Easter faith. With Ascension Day the story shifts its focus. On this day Christ enters glory and commissions the church to be his presence in the world. Jesus in effect says to the church, "You are my body but you are impotent; so wait for the gift of potency, the gift of the Spirit."

On Pentecost, we celebrate the birthday of the church and the coming of the Holy Spirit who empowers the church for mission and ministry. Trinity Sunday ends this season by reminding us that God lives in community, one God in three manifestations: a God who creates, redeems, and perfects human life and social history and who empowers the church to be sacrament in the world. As Christ's presence in the world, the church manifests God's liberating, sacrificial, reconciling, redeeming, transforming love through the Spirit.

The story continues through Ordinary Time, when we tell the story of the struggle to discover what it means to live into our baptism, to become who we already are, to live as if this world is entirely under God's reign.

After six months of living the Easter story, the vision grows dim and we become weary in well-doing. At a time when our wells run dry and we are discouraged both by the darkness of the world and our own souls, Advent tells the story of recapturing lost dreams and preparing for Christ's second coming. Advent is a season of pregnancy, when we prepare for Christ through a change in our perceptions of life. Advent is the season of watching in expectant anticipation, of waiting patiently in hope, of giving up control and opening ourselves to God.

At Christmas we retell the story of the birth of possibilities. We struggle with what it means that Christ has come, Christ is coming, and Christ will come again. Christmas is the story of our not being alone in a world that denies the reality of Easter; it reminds us that God still comes to provide light in our darkness, support in our anxieties, and hope in our despair.

Epiphany focuses on the significance of childhood or, better, childlikeness. It tells the story of our pilgrimage with God in terms of what it means to live as dreamers and visionaries. This is a story of life lived in covenant, a life of show-and-tell. It is acts-evangelism, teaching as Jesus taught by uniting word and deed and providing an example for all to see. Epiphany ends with the story of the price to be paid for such a life and the need for visionaries to acknowledge the presence of evil in the world.

Lent then tells the story of how God grants us the courage to face the principalities and powers in our lives and the world. It is a story of reconciliation and redemption told to those who know that they are continually tempted to deny the truth about themselves and a world under God's rule.

Lent is a time to remember the human condition, the wilderness temptations that confront us, the estrangement we experience from our true selves, the dissonance in our lives, the hungering for wrong things and the need for soul food, the experience of feeling trapped and the need to die to the world's understandings and ways. But always it is the story of God's understanding and grace—acceptance of the unacceptable, forgiving love for the unlovable. Having remembered that part of the story, we are prepared to celebrate once again the story of the Paschal mystery and Easter rebirth.

If a vision of the church year as story is to shape and reshape our lives and form and re-form our community, it will need to be celebrated and lived. It will need to inform every aspect of the church's life and worship. What follows, therefore, are some suggestions for life in a story-formed community.

Eastertide is appropriately a season alive with liturgical celebrations, parish parties, and a festive mood. The Paschal candle rather than the cross leads the procession; the general confession and all kneeling are eliminated; standing for communion is normative; a major gospel procession with incense is proper; and a decorated baptismal font containing water for blessings and reminding us of our baptism dominates the nave.

Parish parties can highlight life in a redeemed community and celebrate the lives of those who manifest the life of the world to come. For example, week one: a party for all those who are engaged in social action for justice and peace (sacrament in the world) and all those engaged in liturgical leadership (lay readers, acolytes, altar guild, etc.). Week two: a party for strangers, neighbors who are not in the parish, street people, the poor and needy, and all newcomers. Week three: a party for all those engaged in shepherding (nurturing and caring) ministries, such as catechists or church school teachers, as well as parish folk who care for the sick, counsel, offer spiritual direction, and so forth, and for those involved in service to the community through soup kitchens, day care centers, and on "hot lines." Week four: a party for all those involved in the administration and organization of parish life, reminding us that to administer means to provide movement toward ministry. And week five: an all-parish family party to celebrate common life in a community of faith where there are no strangers or estranged people.

Once the parties are over, we need to get serious and give extra attention to the reform of parish life and the commitment to ministry in our daily lives. The days between Ascension Day and Trinity Sunday are a time to review seriously, evaluate critically, and plan intentionally for parish life; this is a time to highlight stewardship by celebrating the gifts of the Spirit and eliciting commitments of time, money, and talent for the church's mission and ministry.

During these days each group and person in the church should critically examine involvements and ask to what extent they are helping the church to be the sacrament of Christ, an outward visible manifestation of the gospel in the world. In this way the congregation can prepare for baptisms and individuals can prepare for the renewal of their baptisms at Pentecost. We baptize persons into a community of faith, a community that needs to examine and reform its organizational and communal life at least once each year. There isn't much time.

Assuming we have focused our attention on the necessary reform of our life, Pentecost becomes a festive occasion in which to celebrate new life in the church. The renewal of baptismal covenants and symbolic acts —such as the reading of the gospel and praying the Lord's Prayer (a symbol of Christian life in community) in as many languages as there are nationalities in the congregation—can make this birthday celebration for the church also a commitment to living a new life in the Spirit. Pentecost is a time to celebrate the Spirit's variety of gifts and graces among all of us—children, youth, and adults.

Trinity Sunday is an appropriate time to hold a weekend church fair, with booths to help make everyone aware of the various means of involvement in the church's mission and ministry during the year. Persons can sign up to participate, and workshops can offer an opportunity to acquire the knowledge and skills necessary for these various ministries. In this festive manner, over a weekend the church can prepare to enter Ordinary Time.

This season, which comprises half the church year, provides a time for sustained program and involvement of the community in mission (action, etc.), ministry (education, service, etc.), and worship. This season—even if it is broken up with summer holidays—provides opportunity for events not possible during the rest of the year and offers a chance for growing into the faith through action and reflection.

During this period, persons need to learn to discern God's will for their lives; to be encouraged to integrate their faith and their lives; to be stimulated and equipped for ministry; to grow in their understandings of the Scriptures and the tradition; to be offered experiences of Christian faith and opportunities to reflect on these experiences; to study the social, political, and economic issues which face our world; and to acquire the knowledge and skills necessary both to make complex moral decisions and to influence public policy. It is not a time for the church to slow up its program, but rather a time to develop a sustained program aimed at equipping persons to live their faith day by day.

Advent provides a season for emphasizing solitude and silence, prayer and meditation, inner experience and growth—all of which make outer action and change possible. It is a time to encourage the spiritual life, to slow down parish activity, to teach prayer, and for everyone to attend daily morning and evening prayer. Liturgically this is not a penitential season, so the color blue is more appropriate than purple. It is a season of importance in its own right and not solely related to Christmas.

All unnecessary clutter should be eliminated from the church and a quiet, somber spirit maintained. The festival of St. Nicholas with an exchange of gifts—we hope gifts that will contribute to a better world and be a sign of our Christian life (such as so many hours of care for an elderly person from a youth to his or her parents)

—provides an appropriate interlude in this contemplative season.

Catechesis should focus on the spiritual life, meditation, prayer, and contemplation. All ages need to be introduced to the world of solitude and silence; they need to have their imagination enhanced as well as to find space and time for contemplative activities in this hectic, secular season of parties.

Christmastide is a season to discern where God is and where God is calling us to be. Christmas Eve provides time for a quiet celebration, decorating the church, building a creche, and having a procession to the creche with the figures (minus the wise men, of course), and singing carols. To counter typical Christmas festivities, we can have simple parties for sharing quiet times together and reflecting upon the significance of incarnation and a sacramental view of life. Such activities make a proper movement between Advent and Epiphany.

Epiphany is a season for reflection upon the radical nature of Christian witness. Liturgically the festival of Epiphany is a children's festival of the imagination, a time for adults to recapture their childlike spirits. The blessing of homes and work places can help us understand that the dream has to do with where people live and work.

The Sunday following Epiphany, the baptism of our Lord, provides a major occasion for baptisms and baptismal renewal, a time to remember that we are called to so live that the whole world will know what is true for them also. It is followed by a season focusing parish activity on being Christ's body in the world. For example, it is a time for everyone—children, youth, and adults—to get involved in bearing witness to God's way of conquering evil, by advocating nonviolent resistance as the only way to peace and justice. All parties and activities need to be set aside so that faithful witness to peace through the childlike naivete of power through weakness can dominate parish life. Here learning by doing is appropriate.

Coffee hours after worship should be spent in sharing what is going on outside the church and inviting more people to be involved in mission. It is a season for the discernment of God's will, moral decision making, and action. Education (catechesis) should focus on helping people to engage in mission and ministry.

Lent is a season to reflect on our activity, to get our lives in order, and to prepare the community for Easter baptisms. It is a time to grapple with the human problem and highlight the transformation of our lives through God's grace.

Before the church's penitential season begins, a transition is needed. First, Shrove Tuesday: a rite of reversal, a carnival day of feasting before the fast, a celebration to say farewell to alleluias. Then, Ash Wednesday, a somber day, and Lent begins.

Liturgically, each week of Lent begins with the penitential rite. All flowers and decorations should be removed; candles should be limited to the altar. Purple is the color. Bare wooden crosses should replace the gold crosses in the procession and, if possible, elsewhere. Alleluias are out; silence after the lessons, in. The Way to the Cross can become a weekly devotion. Regular opportunities for the rite of reconciliation and the rite of anointing should be made possible. Kneeling both for prayers and for communion is appropriate. Simple meals and no refreshments at coffee hour now should dominate our style of living.

A total shift in parish life, worship, and the church's environment should provide a time for serious reflection on our life experience, grace and sin, and a concentrated look at the story of salvation, so that we might prepare for Easter baptisms and a new beginning. Lent is the reflective period in the church year, a time when we strive to make sense of our experience and to understand the faith of the church. The season ends with Passion Sunday and the Tenebrae of Holy Wednesday.

I hope these ideas, intended to be suggestive only, have demonstrated how God's story might dominate, direct, and control our life in the church. In order for us to live into our baptism so that God's will is done and God's reign comes, we need to live as a story-formed community of Easter people journeying through time with one another and God.

To be such a community, our liturgical celebrations need to follow more closely God's story and the eternal cycle of the church year; our life together needs to be more supportive of human growth and development; our life in the world needs to be a more dramatic witness to the good news we claim; and our catechetical life needs to bridge our ritual life and daily life, to nurture our community life and prepare us for action in the world.

God's story as re-presented each year within our common life can be an aid in our human pilgrimage. God acts in human history through the passion, death, and resurrection of Jesus Christ, and all life and history are transformed. We live in the joy of that fact and celebrate its reality in our lives. We go forth to live accordingly, ever striving better to discern God's will and understand God's ways that we might better love and serve God.

But while these actions help us to perceive life in new ways, the dream always seems to fade, the vision to weaken, and we get weary of well-doing, we become discouraged with our efforts. So we stop our busyness and turn once again to God. We wait in solitude and silence as we strive to reestablish our relationship with God. Because we do, God comes to us again and reminds us of our calling. We give ourselves wholeheartedly to the manifestations of the vision we bear.

But the principalities and powers in our world and our human weaknesses surface; so we need to admit the brokenness and incompleteness in our lives, turn to God in sorrow, receive God's unmerited, transforming love, and learn how to witness better to God's grace in our lives, to the salvation we know. With our hearts and minds now ready to live into our baptism, we come to celebrate once again the good news of the Easter miracle.

So it is that we journey together in community to actualize the reality of God's good news about human life and history. We are called with God's help to actualize what is already true by ever acknowledging and proclaiming in word and example that God's reign has come, is coming, and is yet to come. Christ has come, Christ is coming, Christ will come again: We live between the here and not yet, as bearers of a story, a memory and a vision, the Good News of God.

4

Worship as Authority for Life and Work

How do we know that the Christian story is true? How do we know that the Christian life is good and right? These and similar questions raise the issue of authority; and about that there seems to be no agreement.

Indeed, the church remains divided over just this issue. Some Christians say our authority for the church's faith and life is the teachings of the Fathers, others the teaching of the magisterium, others in the church's confessions or catechisms, others the Holy Scriptures, and still others the direct inspiration of the Holy Spirit. More serious, the typical church person living in any historic Christian denomination has been so influenced by the modern spirit of individualism and its social expression, relativism, that it is almost impossible for persons in any denomination to reach agreement on what is central and fundamental for religious or moral life. When you bring up the issue of authority, almost everyone becomes uneasy. We no longer have an authoritative tradition. We have lost our corporate moorings and, thus, communal life has been made next to impossible.

Authority has a poor reputation with most of us; liberty is more popular. But liberty that holds authority in contempt is but a mask of self-will. The question, therefore, is not one of authority or no authority but, What is our authority? To what do we give obedience?

To be sure, every person must finally act according to conscience. Even an erroneous conscience must be obeyed. But freedom of conscience without the check of communal authority leads to anarchy. Similarly, blind obedience to authority without the check of individual conscience leads to a tyrannical order.

Communal life requires some authority other than each individual's personal opinion, will, vision, inclination, or taste. Without an agreed upon external authority that calls for the submission and obedience of all persons, community is not possible. Indeed, without an external authority, an act of conscience makes no sense. Yet few in our individualistic world want to live under authority. We are willing to band together in groups as long as our individual consciences can agree, but we are unwilling to submit to any authority outside ourselves. As a result, the community we desire eludes us.

We human beings are religious by nature; that is, we have a need to make sense out of our experiences. As the French phenomenologist Merleau-Ponty stated, "Because we are present to the world, we are condemned to meaning." to live it must have

My life has meaning because I have confidence that at God's command all things came to be: the vast expanse of interstellar space, galaxies, suns, the planets in their courses, and this fragile earth, our island home. From the primal elements God brought forth the human race, formed us in God's image, and blessed us with memory, vision, imagination, sensitivity, reason, and skill so that with God's help we might live in harmony with God within ourselves, with our neighbors, and with all of creation.

We kept betraying God's trust, but God did not abandon us. Through prophets, sages, and priests God called us into covenant, revealed to us the way of life, and

-42-

taught us to hope for salvation. In the fullness of time God came to our aid in Jesus Christ, born of a woman, and made all creation new, opening to us the way of justice and peace, freedom and equity, community and human well-being.

Living as one of us but without sin, Christ gave himself to death so that he might fulfill God's purposes; in raising him from the dead God destroyed the power of evil and brought us out of error into truth, out of sin into righteousness, out of death into life. And that we might live no longer for ourselves, God sent the Holy Spirit to complete God's work in the world and bring to fruition the sanctification of all.

But is this story, paraphrased from an Episcopal Eucharistic prayer, true? How do I know that this story is true? What is my authority for asserting its truth?

If the truth of the Christian faith could be demonstrated by reason alone, the problem of authority would not exist. However, since Christian truth is beyond that which can be demonstrated by logical processes that all reasoning creatures might recognize as valid, the issue of authority is ever before us.

As I have already suggested, Christians have established the authority of their convictions in several different areas, alone or in various combinations and emphases: in Holy Scripture; in tradition as expressed in the creeds and ecumenical councils, the teachings of the magisterium, and the confessions of the church; and in personal experience. However, I for one have never believed the Christian faith true solely because the Bible tells me so, the tradition affirms it, the confessions testify to it, the teachings of the magisterium assert it, or even because my private experience supports it. Rather, I have found the Christian faith to be true because my participation in a story-formed sacramental community has provided me with no reasonable alternative.

-43-

The Christian faith is true for me because I was adopted and inducted into, and nurtured by a community that lives by this faith. I became a conscious Christian when, in full possession and use of my human faculties and in full awareness of other possibilities, I reflected upon my participation in the life of the church and discovered that the only way to make sense of that experience was to commit myself to the faith upon which it is founded.

Simply put, my ability to make a conscious self-commitment to the Christian faith resulted from life in a community of Christian faith. In a world where certainty about ultimate questions is impossible and provable fact is confined, at best, to the vast, but limited area of science, I have discovered that the authority sufficient for making sense out of history and my life is founded in the liturgy—the worship and daily life of a faithful community of faith.

Who would question that our worship influences our beliefs and behaviors and that our beliefs and behaviors influence our worship? Because of this intimate link, the church and its ordained representatives have held authority in liturgical matters. From the beginning the church has contained considerable diversity, and from the beginning it has had to struggle to maintain identity and unity.

Thus, the issue of authority: How do we establish the norms within which diversity is permissible and acceptable, but beyond which none may go without subverting the identity of the community as a whole?

Christian community and authority are dependent upon each other. Christian community is present when persons understand themselves to be persons gathered in response to God's grace, that is, believers in Jesus Christ and members of his church. This self-conscious identity and resulting character provide the basis for

-44-

our common life and norms. This identity and its resultant lifestyle are acquired through participation in a community's rituals or liturgical life. So the church's worship is at the heart of the church's authority, authority necessary for communal life.

In his newest book *The Identity of Christianity*, Anglican priest and Oxford University professor Stephen Sykes searches for an authority in the church that can establish the necessary boundaries for diversity, without which community is not possible. Differences of opinion, he argues, are necessary and natural, and conflict is desirable and inherent in Christian faith. Theology will play a tyrannous part in the resolution of Christian identity unless that identity is strongly maintained by the church in its worship. Doctrine as it proceeds from Scripture, tradition, experience, and reason can become the authority for Christian community only when it is seen in conjunction with other aspects, especially those related to rituals and their social embodiment. For Sykes the authority of the church is, therefore, founded upon the mutual influence of worship and doctrine and provides for diversity and possible change within historical limits and the practical boundaries necessary for communal life.

Geoffrey Wainwright, in his book *Doxology*, imaginatively explores the Latin phrase *lex orandi lex credendi*, or the relationship between the rule of prayer and the rule of belief. I am convinced that it is the church at worship that provides Christians with their authority for faith and life. To be sure, Christians seek to know and do the truth by means of a creative interplay between Scripture, tradition, reason, and experience. Dame Julian of Norwich suggested that authority for the Christian is founded in the common teachings of the church (Scripture and a living tradition of interpretation), natural reason, and the inward, grace-giving operation of the Holy Spirit. But our life as Christians begins when we are adopted into the church, the sacrament of Christ, and when we submit ourselves to its sacraments, for there all are united and one. Within the liturgy we are confronted and engaged by Scripture and tradition. There Christ is present to us as experiencing-reasoning persons, and there we are called to faith and obedience.

Christianity from the very beginning has existed as a corporate reality, as a community. To be Christian means to belong to the community. No one can be Christian alone. To be a Christian means to be adopted into the church through baptism. Personal experience, conviction, or rule of life does not make a person a Christian. Christian existence presumes and implies an incorporation into the body of Christ, a membership in the church. To be baptized is to be Christian; to be baptized is to be a member of the church.

Christianity takes for granted a common life. The church is not merely an association of those who have experienced Christ's saving power, who believe that Jesus is the Christ, or who follow his commandments. The church is a community of persons who abide in Christ's body the church through its sacraments, which continually reveals and seals the communal life of Christians. That is why individual opinions are not of great significance. Christ is revealed not to separated individuals but to the community. Subjectivity and particularism are always a threat to community. Therefore, humbly and trustfully we need to enter the life of the community and seek to find ourselves within it.

The Bible contains all that is necessary for salvation: Nothing that is not contained in the Bible or that cannot be supported by the Bible is *required* for faith. We do not need to supplement Scripture, for it contains the inspired Word (self-revelation) of God in its fullness.

Nevertheless, the Bible is the church's book, a sacred story addressed and entrusted to a community and to persons only insofar as they are members of that community. The Bible was a creation of the community; the Scripture has authority in the church because the church acknowledges its authority. The Bible contains a message from God, but it is the faithful community that receives, acknowledges, testifies to, and interprets its truth. The sacred character of the Bible is verified by the faith of the community. The book and the church cannot be separated; only within the church can the Bible be truly understood.

Scripture needs to be explained. This is made possible through the medium of a faithful community. Scripture is complete, but it does not claim to be self-sufficient. If we say that the Bible is self-sufficient, we expose it to subjective, arbitrary interpretation, cutting away its sacred source. The community of faith comes first. The gospel was revealed first in the life of the community and its sacraments. Later the gospel was recorded in the Scriptures and made canon by the community.

It still occurs in that order. We come to the church not because we have faith but because we desire it and know it can be ours only if we live in a community of faith. We come to the church not because we understand Scripture but because we want to, and because we know that if we are to understand, we will need the help of the community which made it holy. In the experience of Christ at baptism, in the Eucharist, and in the other sacraments, Christians come to know the Christ of Scripture and are thereby enabled to make sense of the Gospels.

Interpretation of Scripture has been a burning issue throughout the history of the church. Many appeal to Scripture, but as St. Hilary of Poitiers, the great defender of orthodoxy, wrote in the fourth century, "Scripture is not in the reading, but in the understanding" (De Trinitate). Scripture belongs to the church·

only in the community can Scripture be adequately understood and correctly interpreted. That is why Tertullian insisted on the *regula fidei*, the rule of faith, as the necessary key to interpreting the Scripture. And this rule of faith, the apostolic message or *kerygma* contained in the Creed of the Apostles, became the church's baptismal creed. Apart from this rule, Scripture could be misunderstood. So Scripture and tradition were indivisibly intertwined from the very beginning.

The church does not judge Scripture, but the church is the keeper and guardian of the divine truth stored in it, and the apostolic tradition provides an indispensible guide for understanding Scripture and the ultimate warrant for right interpretation. At our baptism we are initiated into this rule of faith. Through the continuing renewal of our baptism and profession, we increase our commitment of faith. Tradition, therefore, is a hermeneutical principle and method, providing a living context and comprehensive perspective through which the church's book, the Bible, can be rightly interpreted and grasped.

Still, God's self-disclosure—the firsthand experience of God—is available to all persons. This experience of God we make real and celebrate in the church's sacraments. To be Christian is not to know all about Christ but to live in relationship to Christ. This living experience supports and informs our lives. But individual experience not tested and confirmed by the community can be misleading and dangerous. Just as discernment of the spirits is an essential aspect of spiritual direction and the life of prayer, so all our religious experience needs to be evaluated by the community.

In the midst of the Great Awakening, Jonathan Edwards, the eighteenth-century New England divine, wrote *A Treatise Concerning the Religious Affections*. It was his hope that the church would adopt his criteria for a true religious experience—for example, significant change in moral behavior. While he acknowledged that the experience of God is part of God's continuing relationship with creation, Edwards also recognized that the judgment of the community and the use of reason are necessary to protect us from error and self-deception. Indeed, in his list of tests for the validity of religious experience, Edwards included an increase in intellectual understanding.

The community's use of reason is an essential aspect of authority. The church puts confidence in the human mind through its intuitive and intellectual powers to discern truth, goodness, and beauty. Behind this contention is the conviction that the created order reflects the mind of God that, in turn, is discernable to human reason. To put it another way, by using our corporate reasoning we participate in the mind of God.

This view is the basis for what is called natural theology, the teaching that all humankind can know God by observing the natural world and human beings. Such a perspective implies, of course, that philosophy and the sciences provide a source for knowledge of God. Reason alone cannot bring wholeness or provide all knowledge. But there is no radical discontinuity between God and God's creation: God is immanent as well as transcendent. The community that holds Scripture, tradition, and experience as authoritative dimensions of community life should encourage persons to ask searching questions and pursue truth relentlessly. For ultimately this quest will open them to the mind of God.

Responding to a young poet who had been moved by a university lecture she gave, writer Flannery O'Connor wrote:

> One result of the stimulation of your intellectual life that takes place in college is a shrinking of the imaginative life. Don't get so entangled with intellectual pursuits that you miss the experience of truth. The intellectual difficulties have to be met,

however, and you will be meeting them the rest of your life. If you want faith, you have to work for it. It is a gift, but for very few is it a gift without any demand for equal time devoted to its cultivation. To find out about faith you have to go to the most intellectual believers. God has given us reason and it can lead us toward a comprehension of the truth revealed to us in the experience of the Eucharist. Christian faith is no leap into the absurd. I find it reasonable to believe even though these convictions are beyond reason.

You see, I believe what the church teaches—that God has given us reason to use and it can lead us toward a knowledge of him, through analogy; that he has revealed himself in history and continues to do so through the church, and that he is present (not just symbolically) in the Eucharist on our altars. (*The Habit of Being: The Letters of Flannery O'Connor*, edited by Sally Fitzgerald, New York, Vintage Books, 1980, p. 476 f.)

What O'Connor realized was that through the use of his reasoning abilities, the young man would ultimately be led to an experience of truth.

But the question remains. How can Scripture, tradition, experience, and reason be orchestrated to produce an authoritative position? The answer, I believe, is to be found in the church councils: when representatives from the clergy and laity of the church's numerous faith communities gather to reflect—in the light of tradition and contemporary experience and through the use of reason—and thereby arrive at consensus.

In such a way the church speaks with authority, and each of us is to listen to its call to obedience, evoking individual conscience only as a last resort. It is my belief that the most important act the church in council takes is the ordering of worship. Agreement on worship is essential for community life, because common worship is the final source of authority for faith and life. In worship we continually attempt to open ourselves to God so that we might be obedient to God's will and walk in God's ways.

I am reminded of the process for preparing adults for Holy Baptism in the new rite in the Episcopal *Book of Occasional Services*. At the Sunday Eucharist when the catechumens are admitted, the celebrant asks, "What do you seek?" The catechumens reply, "Life in Christ"— that is, life in the church, life in this story-formed sacramental community. The catechumens are then asked three questions: "Do you accept the two great commandments to love God and neighbor? Do you promise to regularly participate in the church's worship? And do you intend to open yourselves to the Word of God, that is, to the experience of the Gospel?"

Sponsors representing the community then promise to support the catechumens by their prayers and example so that they might grow in the knowledge and love of God. The community prays that the catechumens may be granted the power of the Holy Spirit to persevere in their intentions and grow in faith and understanding. They are then signed with the cross. Thus they begin a lengthy period of regular participation in the worshiping community, in the practice of life in accordance with the gospel, especially ministry to the poor and neglected, and in learning the story of salvation as revealed in Holy Scripture.

After a lengthy period of participation in the cultic life of a Christian community, catechumens are encouraged to become candidates for baptism. But only during this next stage of preparation do they engage in theological reflection on their experiences in the church. First comes the experience, and then the reflective explanation and interpretation.

-51-

Experience LX

Cyril, the bishop of Jerusalem during the fourth century, advised baptismal candidates, who had been participating in the cultic life of the church for up to three years, not to share with anyone what he was to tell them. "When this instruction is over, if any catechumen tries to get out of you what your teachers have told you, tell nothing, for they are outside the mystery that we have delivered to you. . . . Guard the mystery, for if a catechumen hears something divulged that he has not experienced, he will not comprehend and thereby will think nothing of the whole matter, scoffing at what he has been told" (*Catechetical Lectures*). Cyril knew that catechumens cannot comprehend what they had not first participated in and experienced.

However, on the basis of these participatory experiences within the community, the catechumens also needed help in reflecting on their experiences and framing an intellectual understanding of the church's faith and life. Through this twofold process it became possible for the catechumen to make a profession of faith, an affirmation of the truth as expressed in the church's baptismal creed.

Without meaning, life ceases to exist. Without claims of truth, meaning is impossible. To say that something is meaningful is to describe how it helps us to understand life and our lives; to say that something is true is to claim that it reveals to us the very ground in which our lives are rooted and makes life not only understandable, but worth living.

But the church does not own the truth. God's Spirit works in the world as well as the church. The church claims only that it offers an experience and expression of the truth to those who participate in its life.

Truth is judged by the fruit it bears in the lives of those who claim it. Ultimately, we all must live with uncertainty: Life is risk. We bet our lives that the way we perceive life and our own lives and the resultant way we live is wiser and better than any other. The test is in the living. We simply have to be content with affirming a way of faith and life that cannot lay claim to absolute certainty.

And so, at the close of this chapter on truth and authority, we recall Pilate's question to Jesus, "What is truth?" (John 18:38). In a world of many truths and half truths he was hungry for truth itself or, failing that, at least for the truth that there is no truth. All of us are like Pilate in our asking after truth, but the truth we desire cannot be stated. Truth simply is; so Jesus stands there in silence and lets the silence speak: "Truth is something words cannot tell but only tell about."

But having experienced truth, we find ourselves longing to tell the truth or to put some words around the silence that is truth. Still, all we ultimately have to tell is a story that each week as a community we re-present in our ritual. More important, our participation in this communal story through the sacraments reveals truth, truth that makes sense of all the agonies and ecstasies of our lives.

In the last analysis, this truth, which becomes truth for us and provides us with those convictions that make our lives meaningful, is founded in the authority of liturgy, the cultic and daily life of a story-formed, faithful, worshipping community. Without a common authority there is nothing to bind us together or aid us to live life in common. A common authority is necessary for the gift of community. Our authority is based upon common liturgy that celebrates and makes present a common memory and vision.

The implications should be obvious. Worship, for all ages, must be at the heart of the church's life. The church needs to order its liturgical life, and congregations must order their life of worship, accordingly. Further, the Christian story as contained in the Scripture must be known and internalized. The Christian tradition as contained in the creeds and early councils of the church must be known and internalized. The Christian experience of the Triune God must be made known and discerned. Human reason must be developed and critically employed to interpret Scripture in the light of the tradition and contemporary experience. But first we must agree on the nature and character of authority in the church and commit ourselves to it.

5

Reclaiming Worship as the Heart of the Community

Rituals are a community's repeated symbolic actions expressing its memory and vision. Rituals are at the center of human life, binding together past, present, and future. Without meaningful and purposeful rituals, daily life cannot be made or kept fully human. Humanizing rituals humanize all of life. When we do not feel comfortable participating in a group's rituals, we do not feel at home in the group. Conflicting rituals result in alienation, meaningless rituals in dehumanization. On the other hand, common meaningful rituals result in the gift of community.

Cultic life, however, is complicated. In *Real Presence*, Regis Duffey tells about a work Leonard Bernstein composed for the opening of the Kennedy Center in Washington, D.C., in which the text of the Latin Mass was set to music. However, each Latin text was followed by songs in English explaining why it is difficult to believe the truth that the Mass text proclaims. While the Latin text suggested the possibilities of ritual and worship, the English text suggested the problems of belief and response.

Bernstein knew that the texts and the rituals belong to a community and not simply to individuals. As Bernstein's Mass begins, a young man in blue jeans is donning the vestments of celebration while people gather around him. These people have all the appearances of a

Christian community. But then comes Bernstein's apt reworking of the Pauline axiom (1 Corinthians 10:17): "Because we eat the one bread, we are not necessarily one at all." Pauline unity and community are not the result of hymns sung in unison, Bernstein seems to be saying; for, as Bernard Lonergan reminds us, community is the achievement of common meaning.

As the Mass proceeds, we see that there are only private meanings among groups of individuals who prefer ceremonies to the mystery of Christ's presence, songs and dances to the experiences to the truth. To illustrate this point, Bernstein climaxes his work by having the celebrant stand above the congregation (like Moses on the mountain) holding the symbols of Christ's presence. Down below the people are carousing, much as the Israelites did in the episode of the golden calf (Exodus 32-35). The celebrant hurls down the symbols of Christ's presence among people who are not really present. In the monologue that follows, he comments on the fragility of ritual and the weakness of people who do not really live in community.

Bernstein's observations are correct. Both we and our rituals are fragile. Nevertheless, I contend that participation in a faithful community at worship is essential if we are to experience the truth of the gospel.

Daily life provides the context for expressing the truth we have experienced through cultic life. Jesus asked, "Who do you say that I am?" The disciples had shared an intuitive experience of life with Jesus, but Jesus wanted to know if they made any rational sense of it. Jesus, therefore, praised Peter, who arrives at the intellectual conclusion, "You are the Christ" (Matthew 6:13-16).

While dependent upon the intuitive experience of Jesus, we express the truth of Jesus doctrinally through an intellectual act. Truth as making sense of our lives is a result of objective reflection on subjective experience within a story-formed, sacramental community. For whom is the gospel truth? Simply for those who in their search for meaning are willing to engage in the difficult work of reflecting on their experience of participation in the church's worship.

The discovery of the gospel's truth necessitates risk and points us to journey down a dark and dangerous road. We are called to bet our very lives that one way of perceiving and living life is wiser than another.

Coming from the Greek word for public service (*leitourgia*), the word "liturgy" has become associated with the rites (texts) and ceremonies (actions) of public worship. Nevertheless, liturgy best refers to the activities of a people bound together in a story-formed, sacramental community, activities that include both cultic life (ritual celebrations) and daily life.

Our worship should make a difference in our personal and social history. The problem, however, is that it often does not. For example, why is it that our celebration of the Eucharist does not necessarily result in the transformation of human experience and history— that is, in living the Eucharist?

A community's cultic life is comprised of symbols, myths, and rituals. Cultic life shapes a person's perceptions or faith, makes possible personal and communal experience of the "divine," and forms that person's character, that is, his or her identity, orientation to life, and dispositions toward behavior.

Rituals are repetitive, symbolic actions that express a community's myth or sacred story. Intensification, or communal, rites follow the calendar, binding a people into community, establishing meaning and purpose for the lives of its members, and both sustaining and transmitting to the next generation its world view and value system. Transition rites, of passage and initiation, aid in understanding and accepting change during life-cycle movements.

Healthy personal and social life necessitates a positive link between cultic and daily life. We move from daily life to cultic life and from cultic life to daily life. In *The Dynamics of Religion*, Anglican priest and sociologist Bruce Reed images life as an oscillation of persons back and forth between what he calls extra-dependence and intra-dependence. Cultic life or worship properly focuses our dependent needs for meaning on God (extra-dependence) and thereby provides inner strength (intra-dependence) for purposeful life in society.

We humans are dependent beings. Meaningful and purposeful life is comprised of interdependent relationships with other persons and an absolute dependence upon God. At worship we consciously focus on our dependent relationship with God. Through the week, we live in an unconscious reliance upon God. As we live day by day, we become conscious of our limits, brokenness, and incompleteness. We return to the church to participate in its cultic life, which can reestablish our dependence upon God, transform us, and empower us to return to the daily round.

Of course, the key to the oscillation process is the authenticity of worship and the connections it makes with daily life. At least in theory there should be correspondence between our worship and our lives. Nevertheless, the two are sometimes estranged.

Why is this so? While the reasons are numerous, five immediately come to mind.

1. *Psychosocial Pathologies.* Persons may participate in a community's cultic life in unhealthy ways. Religion is both natural and necessary for human life, but the human longing for religious meaning can express itself in both negative and positive ways. Some religion is inclined to support health, other to support sickness.

An estrangement between cultic and daily life may exist when people either produce a pathological split between the sacred and the secular or maintain a pathological approach to the use of ritual for escape. An example would be if ritual were understood as magic or the means to convince God to do something God would not do without that person's convincing. It is a coercive, manipulative understanding of ritual whereby a person seeks to control life for his or her purposes.

2. *Conflicting Rituals, World Views, and Value Systems.* We live in a complex and diversified culture. We are also exposed to a variety of rituals, each intended to influence our understandings and ways of life. Each day we are confronted with conflicting world views and value systems, each aimed at gaining our loyalty. The fact that we participate in the church's cultic life is no guarantee that it will be the fundamental influence in our lives. For some, the church's cultic life will be so central to their being that their participation in other rituals will have minimal effect. For others, the church's cultic life will be peripheral, and other rituals will significantly influence their world views and value systems.

In our complex culture effective patterns of enculturation are difficult to establish. Toleration is great, and the range of acceptable rituals, world views, and value systems tends to produce a cultural relativism. As a result, the church's cultic life is less successful in influencing daily life than it was in a simpler, more homogeneous culture.

In the course of life a person in our culture will participate in many diverse rituals, some of which will express radically divergent world views and value systems. There are political rituals such as peace marches and political party dinners; there are economic rituals such as labor strikes and office parties; there are civic rituals such as Mardi Gras and the Fourth of July; there are school rituals such as commencement and the Friday beer blast; there are entertainment rituals such as movies and the disco; there are television rituals such as the "soaps" and advertisements; and, perhaps most powerful and significant, there are sports rituals such as the Super Bowl. (In most cultures sporting events are important cultic acts; this may help to explain why a catechumen in the early church was required to avoid the "public games.")

The diversity of rituals in which people participate makes it difficult to evaluate the influence of the church's cultic life. The world views and value systems sustained by the culture inform a person's experience of the cultic life of the church and thereby diminish its power. The variety of legitimated rituals present in the culture produces a relativism that diminishes the influence of any one ritual on the lives of its participants.

3. Cultural Pluralism and Cultic Inadequacies. North American culture is so much a part of our lives that we are unaware of it until we find ourselves in another culture. A visit to Latin America, Africa, or Asia often produces culture shock. We forget, however, that there are numerous cultural distinctions to be found here. Some are regional: There is a significant difference between Southern culture and that of the West Coast. Some are ethnic: There is a difference between Mexican-Americans in Texas and Vietnamese-Americans in New York. Some are racial: There is a difference between black and white culture. Some are socio-economic: There is a difference between the rich and the poor. And so on. What are obvious, accepted, and expected understandings and ways of perceiving, behaving, and becoming in one group are strange and confusing in another. While all of us in the United States share a common culture, we exemplify tremendous cultural differences.

We have created a cultic life that is sometimes too unrelated to the culture and sometimes too much in harmony with it. The Eucharist must be celebrated within some cultural expression. The question is, To what extent should the church respect a people's culture and adapt the ritual to its cultural ways?

Ritual in the Catholic church during the baroque period reflected the European culture of the time. The Eucharist became a triumphalistic, ecclesiastical concert and theatrical display in festive halls of grandeur. At the same time the intransigence of the Tridentine liturgical practice excluded almost every possibility of adapting the liturgy to other cultures, thus inflicting the European cultural experience on every corner of the globe. An exception that proves the generalization was the rites controversy in China, where the Jesuits adapted the ritual to the culture.

If cultic life and daily life are to correspond, we must discover a way to keep the universal character of the Christian faith while at the same time making it relevant to the particularities of each culture. Some adaption of cultic life to the culture is necessary, but that adaption must at the same time make possible the transformation of culture. When these attempts are inadequate, they result in a split between the celebrating and living of the Eucharist.

4. *Cultic Shallowness.* Cultic life is essentially an intuitive, imaginative activity in the arena of aesthetic sensibility. Knowing is tacit and personal, encompassing "mystical" experience. There are states of insight into the depths of reality that cannot be plumbed by discursive logic. Such illuminations and revelations, while essentially nonrational, are not irrational, romantic, or unreal.

Enlightenment Christianity with its concern for the intellect and morality has sometimes been insensitive to experience and the affections. It has on occasion ignored the fact that we cannot make sense of what we have not experienced. It has tended to forget that daily

life as ministry needs to be rooted in the experience of
God in Christ; ministry is a projection of that experience. When the experience is lacking, the resultant
meaning and ministry are lost.

The late anthropologist Margaret Mead suggested
that Christian rituals are designed to re-present the affections identified with the primal event of Christ's life,
death, and resurrection. Every ritual is properly an an-
amnesis. Ritual is a bundle of symbols, symbolic acts,
and symbolic narrative intended to transport the par-
ticipant into the reality to which they point. The reen-
actment of the community's primal event is intended to
draw participants more closely into union with Christ
and thereby affect their daily lives.

Religious experience is considered rare in our culture
because we have made so little of the imagination, won-
der, and our intuitive way of knowing. We humans are
not just creatures who think analytically and logically.
We also have a capacity to see behind and beyond the
surface of life, to participate in its depth.

Our cultic life for too long has been dominated by the
discursive, the rationalistic, and the prosaic. Good ritual focuses primarily on the role of the symbolic and the
pre-rational. This is not to defend a shallow asceticism
or emotionalism but to suggest that our rituals are often
characterized by too much discussion and talk, stereo-
typed actions, mundane music, naturalistic art,
unimaginative drama, and lack of dance.

Good ritual should awaken the artistic consciousness.
The story we re-present through music, dance, drama,
poetry, painting, and sculpture should touch our human story in its depths and illumine its meaning. Religion is indeed danced before it is believed. Religious
experience begins at the level of symbol, myth, and
ritual, rather than as signs, concepts, or reflective actions; religion begins with the affections, not intellectual conviction.

Far too many people have been victimized by a false religion of subjective emotionalism devoid of both thinking and imagination; nevertheless, intellectuals would do well to remember that in our scientific age we have by and large lost contact with the dimensions of reality that give rise to the religious.

When our cultic life is inadequate—that is, when our cultic life is not focused on intuitive knowing and when the quality of the intuitive experience is mundane—it cannot provide the necessary foundation for faithful daily life.

5. *Cultic Ineffectiveness.* When the Hebrew prophets denounced the Israelites' worship, it was because it belied their conduct. The prophets did not reject ritual, only its misuse. And the reason was clear: It did not result in proper moral life. A similar theme is reflected in the teachings of Jesus. Perhaps that helps to explain why in the history of the church, whenever the community discerned that it was not living the Eucharist, it sought to reform its celebration of the Eucharist. Indeed, the history of the church can be best understood from the perspective of liturgical reform. The Reformation/Counter-Reformation period of history is a good example.

Insofar as the celebration of the Eucharist fails to produce appropriate fruit in the lives of participants, the ritual needs to be examined to see whether it is a faithful expression of the belief system. As this has been done in our own day, significant reforms have been made.

For example, the old ritual may have supported a split between word and deed. The lack of preaching or poor preaching among Roman Catholics and the neglect of the Eucharist among Protestants may have established and reinforced a functional separation between cultic and daily life. The renewed emphasis among all Christians on word *and* sacrament is intended to create harmony between celebrating the Eucharist and living the Eucharist.

Likewise, while Protestants tended to ignore the church year, Roman Catholics typically used the church year for doctrinal purposes. The nature of myth as sacred story and the integration of the story with our story was for all intents and purposes lost. The reform in the lectionary and a new attention to living the cycle of the ritual as an expression of the human spiritual pilgrimage are attempts at a new synthesis of cultic and daily life.

And for too long both Protestants and Roman Catholics worshiped as observers at a ritual controlled by the clergy. Protestants came to hear a good sermon and choir, Roman Catholics to see Jesus. Such behaviors reinforced the idea that Christians held faith at a distance and did not participate in it or act upon it. The new rituals demand participation and, we hope, will help people to make consistent their celebration and their daily life.

Typically, in the past persons attended worship as individuals. While the ritual provided a place to pray one's own prayers and encouraged private, pietistic actions, it ignored the social dimensions of human life. The communal nature of the new Eucharistic ritual attempts to change that behavior.

In addition, the old Eucharistic ritual was highly penitential. The ritual reinforced a negative view of the self and its potential. Persons typically came away understanding themselves essentially as sinners, miserable worms, unworthy messes, rather than as a redeemed people. Each week worshipers returned to get enough grace to make it through another week, but rarely did they leave believing that they had the power to make a significant difference in the world. For many the sacrament was understood as bestowing grace.

Author Tad Guzie makes the important point that the sacrament is not an encounter that gives grace, but an opportunity for people already in God's grace to celebrate that fact. Too many Christians come to the sacrament to get something denied them in daily life, rather than to celebrate and make real the truth of God's grace already present and active in every aspect of their daily lives.

At the close of the old rite, people were simply dismissed. Now, having been fed in the Eucharist, they are sent forth to love and serve the Lord. This renewed apostolic understanding of life attempts to move people from celebrating the Eucharist to living a Eucharistic life.

Our cultic life is judged by the fruit it bears in daily life. The process of keeping the two in harmony is never ending. It is necessary to reform our cultic life continually so that it corresponds with our understanding of Christian daily life.

The necessity of cultural adaptation has some very practical implications for the Christian community. First, we need translations of the texts into the language of the people.

Second, we must have music with quality and diversity—classical style, folk idiom, and Afro-American, Asian, and Hispanic beats, tones, and rhythms—to bring the text to life for its participants.

Third, the architecture, iconography, and dress need to be in harmony with both a people's culture and the historic period in which a community finds itself. Reproductions of churches built during the Middle Ages in Europe, in colonial New England, or in the nineteenth century are no longer acceptable even if they are affordable. Vestments created for survival in cold temperatures are ludicrous in a hot climate. Sacred images need to represent both the particularity of a culture and the universality of the God to which they point. Folk art also needs to be encouraged.

Fourth, while the shape or structure of the ritual needs to be maintained, the symbols and symbolic actions used need to be in harmony with the culture. For example, the kiss of peace, symbolizing that in the church there are no strangers or people estranged from each other, is essential to the liturgy; but the symbolic expression of that kiss needs to be in harmony with the culture. In our culture both men and women hug to make up and hug close friends.

In general, Christians traveling from church to church ought to be aware that the Eucharist is being celebrated and easily recognize where in the shape of the liturgy (the order of worship) the people are, so that they may participate with their own cultural words and symbolic action.

In addition to cultural adaptation, we need ritual reform. First, if word and sacrament are to be effectively united, preaching needs to be radically improved. An effective sermon needs to bring together the people's story and the community's sacred story; it should move the community to the sacrament where the life, death, and resurrection of Jesus Christ can be made present to their lives, and then lead them out to proclaim by word and example the Good News of God in Christ.

Second, the ritual must encourage full participation of all the people. This means returning the preparation and celebration of the ritual to the people. This also implies the welcoming of women to the ordained priesthood.

Third, a sense of community must be manifest. We need to emphasize the kiss of peace. All the people need to share a common loaf of "real bread" consecrated and broken, as well as a common cup. In this regard, music and dance need to become more communal and less a production by choirs and dance groups.

Fourth, we need to establish a balance between a redeemed and a penitential community, forbidding prayers of confession during Eastertide and making them mandatory only during Lent. Penitence needs to be put within a redeemed context, so that people might learn that their sin is a denial of their true humanity and potential, not a statement about their essential human condition.

Fifth, the ritual needs to celebrate an apostolic community—to bring the human condition and world experience into worship and then send participants forth to love and serve the Lord by seeking peace and justice.

Sixth, the ritual needs to make much better use of the arts and involve all of the senses (taste, touch, smell, sound, and sight). We need to make dance more natural (religion is danced before it is believed), music more central (the creed is more of a love song than an affirmation of intellectually held convictions), drama more significant, and language more poetic. Both the immanent and transcendent natures of God need to be expressed and experienced.

If the ritual becomes too otherworldly, it becomes quietist and escapist. If the ritual becomes too this-worldly, it becomes moralistic and humanistic. If the ritual becomes too intellectual, it suffers from rationalism; if it becomes too emotional, it suffers from pietism. The solution balances these elements.

In any case, ritual is at the heart of the church's life; nothing is more important. In 1925 Willard Sperry, dean of the Harvard Divinity School and minister to the University, argued that the church shares religious tasks with many other institutions, but the conduct of public worship is its distinctive and unique responsibility. Wherever and whenever persons meet for worship, he said, there is a church, clearly and distinctly defined. Everything else may be conceded or shared.

If the church does nothing else for the world than to keep open a house—symbolic of the homeland of the human soul—where persons come together for cultic life, it is doing both persons and the social order the greatest possible service, and nothing can compare with it. As long as the church bids people to come and worship and provides a credible vehicle for worship, it need not question its place, mission, or influence on the world.

6

A Common Life
to Support
an Alternative Consciousness

A community of faith assumes and requires a particular character of shared life. While Christian community is formed by a story that communicates shared memory and vision, while the authority for the truth of this story is made known through the community's corporate worship, and while participation in the community's liturgical life is necessary if its story is to inform people's faith and life, shared experience in a particular sort of community is necessary both to sustain and nurture this alternative consciousness in the world and to provide a witness to that consciousness.

The church is a human association of a particular kind. It is not a "natural" group like a biological family; it is not a group based solely on common interests like a club; it is not a provider of goods and services like a corporation; it is not a voluntary association to meet and protect the interests of its members like the American Medical Association. The church is the *ekklesia* of God, a gathering of people called out to be something and do something together on behalf of everyone: a covenant community whose purpose is to serve others.

The church as the body of Christ is first of all a community, a particular sort of community. As a community of faith, the church focuses its attention on every aspect of life—the religious, social, political, and economic; it calls for the involvement of the total personality; it involves life shared in the depths of joy and sorrow, pain and pleasure; it regulates its life implicitly by custom and hence does not require explicit by-laws; it requires that obligations to each other include whatever love demands, the very opposite of contractual relationships; and it proclaims that the participants' worth is not judged by what they contribute or how much they participate but only as a consequence of their being: Each person is of value and none is of greater worth.

The church, the body of Christ, is a sacramental community, a visible manifestation of an invisible reality. Stories are comprised of words that name experiences; sacraments are actions that re-present those experiences. Stories are told *in* community, sacraments are actions performed *by* a community. Sacraments make real rather than make true; that is, the sacraments are not essential for receiving God's revelation or grace. This revelation and grace are already present in the world, but this revelation of God and God's grace are celebrated in the sacraments. We celebrate what is, thereby both making us aware of it and making it real for ourselves.

In the early days of the church Jesus' followers were not preoccupied with *ideas* about him. They mainly wanted to tell the *story* of their experience of him, a story that makes contact with the human story and provides a basis for making sense of it. Similarly, the sacraments are actions we perform as community in order to make the truth it proclaims real in our lives.

The church as sacrament is a sign and witness to the truth of Christ, a spiritual truth that requires incarnation for it to be true. Jesus began his ministry by spreading the word that God's long-awaited and longed-for rule had begun. Of course, that rule wasn't any more obvious then than it is now, so what people needed to do was repent—that is, change their perception of reality and behave accordingly. Only the eyes of faith, said Jesus, can make the invisible visible, and only those who risk living as if it is true will ever know if it is.

As Jesus went about spreading this word, he gathered students. One day, says the story (Mark 1:21-22), while he was conducting a class in the local synagogue, a group gathered to listen. What Jesus had to say was startling. But what everyone noticed was that he was a teacher who didn't just talk. His actions and his words were consistent. That was strange, of course; for then, as now, most people who teach tell students to do as they say and not as they do.

Consequently, most of the students were truly impressed, though they still wondered at Jesus' words. New truth is never easy to grasp, let alone accept. Still, here was a teacher who provided in his own life evidence to support his lectures; here was a teacher, therefore, who had authority.

Jesus, of course, is the supreme example of how the church as sacrament is to embody the stories it tells; by uniting word and deed it establishes the authority for the truth it proclaims. By becoming sacrament in the world it offers the world an alternative consciousness.

The church is in the world. The world is in the church. The church is not all good and the world totally evil; the church is not always faithful and the world consistently unfaithful; the church is not always wise and the world invariably foolish; the church does not always know God's will or live in harmony with God's will while the world is ever ignorant of or estranged from God's will.

Obviously, however, neither is the converse true. The church must be careful neither to identify completely with the world nor wholly to stand over against it. The church is called to be in the world, but not become of it. The real issue for the church is being a faithful community. Out of this faithfulness will come either an affirmation or judgment of the world's ways.

To be a faithful community we as church need first of all to turn our attention from what we should do and say in the world to who and whose we are. Both character and conscience are aspects of the moral life. But the modern church, so concerned with conscience questions of what is the right thing to do, has forgotten that it is as believers in Jesus Christ and members of his church that we ask, What is the right thing to do?

In his insightful book *Prophetic Imagination*, theologian Walter Brueggemann suggests that the church is to be a community with an alternative perception (way of seeing, which is faith) and consciousness (way of being, which is identity) to the perception and consciousness of the dominant culture and thereby be an agent in the transformation of culture. The purpose of the church is to reveal an alternative way of perceiving and living life.

The relationship between American culture and Christianity, past and present, is extremely complex. Perhaps all American Christians can agree upon is that we live in an age characterized by a crisis in identity. Increasingly people are asking, What has it meant and what should it mean in the future to be an American, to be a Christian? This may not be a new situation, and surely there are some who believe the answer is obvious. Still it appears as if once again the church is at a turning point in its life.

While some debate whether Americans have ever lived within a Christian ethos (a distinguishing Christian character and common guiding beliefs), most observers agree that there is no Christian ethos informing the country's common life now and no likelihood that one will emerge in the near future.

American culture (the shared, learned understandings and ways of life or common world view, value systems, and patterns of behavior) has from the beginning been founded upon the principle of pluralism. That is, our culture is committed to the maintenance of diverse subcultures and identity-conscious communities, living in openness to each other. While periodically some persons dream of a melting pot for the blending of diversity into commonness and others dream of a "civil religion" to unite us, the principle of political pragmatism upon which our nation was founded has subverted the dream.

In our history, at times the concern for identity has been so dominant that we feared the dissolution of our common life; at other times the concern for openness has been so dominant that we have feared the dissolution of our separate communities. Within this complex and pluralistic American culture some churches—or better, some expressions of the church—have sought to identify with the culture and hence lost their distinctive identities, while others have attempted to separate themselves from the culture and hence lost their ability to influence our common life. The goal—to remain in-but-not-of the culture so as to be a constant force of transformation—has been difficult to realize.

Christian faith may have played a significant role in shaping the United States, but even from its beginnings the nation has supported extremely diverse understandings of Christian faith. We have cultivated pluralism even among those who claim Jesus Christ as sovereign. Religious fervor has dried up on numerous occasions only to be renewed again, but our struggle with faithfulness in a pluralistic church, culture, and world, while varying in intensity, has remained constant. And once again, at this juncture in time, we seem to be asking the old but ever-new question, What does it

mean to be the church of Jesus Christ and how can we ⚡
be faithful in our day?

The problem with the contemporary church is that it
is so enculturated to the American ethos that it has little
power to transform the culture. The culture expects
that its religious communities will support and bless it,
but the church is intended to be an alternative community with a counterconsciousness, in-but-not-of the
world, acting for the transformation of that culture.
The church has a tendency to become so enculturated
(we might say successful, in cultural terms) that it loses
its identity and vitality, its prophetic imagination and
purpose.

But until it regains its identity, the church will lack
the power to fulfill its mission. How can the church
regain its lost identity? First of all by getting its story
straight. All communities are story-formed; without a
story there is no corporate vitality. If a community's
story is not known and believed, nothing it does will
make any difference. For a Christian that story is centered in the Paschal mystery of Holy Week. This is a
culturally subversive story, but it can be distorted to
support the status quo when it focuses on individual
souls and life in the hereafter for those who are saved
from this sinful world.

Therefore, the story needs to be complemented by
the visionary imagination of the prophet. The prophet,
at home in the memory of the true story, senses its
distortions and, through a poetic appeal to the imagination, nurtures and evokes a vision of the alternative
future that is the fulfillment of the community's story.
Thus the prophet makes possible the transformation of
the consciousness. Together the story of the priest and
the word of the prophet unite to shape a counterconsciousness that makes possible the formation of an alternative community whose life is a critique of the dominant culture and the example of an alternative.

how they start

If we can change a people's consciousness, we can change the world. A changed consciousness is more radical than any attempt at political or economic change and more profound than all effort at social action. Through alternative communities that manifest a counterconsciousness, the church can contribute to the transformation of culture.

The mission of the church is determined by its origin. The church does not generate its own mission; it participates in God's mission to the world. In this sense it can be said that the church does not *have* a mission, it *is* mission. And God's mission is to bring to fulfillment the new humanity and new world inaugurated through the life, death, and resurrection of Jesus Christ. The church participates in this mission by being a sign of and a witness to this yet-to-be-actualized new reality.

As of Good Friday-Easter, all humanity is re-established in relation to God, and all the world is placed under God's gracious rule. The power of evil is overcome. We humans are made whole and holy. The world is made peaceful and just.

Our sin is that we do not perceive the world and people in this manner. Our consciousness is distorted, so we do not act as if the gospel is true. If everyone could see the truth of the new reality and act accordingly, the truth of salvation for all persons and the world would be actualized. The church is called to manifest and herald this radical consciousness by foolishly living in its truth. For only then will others be able to recognize the truth the church proclaims, change the way they perceive reality, and act accordingly.

Yet even as we describe the church's mission and our American culture today, we are aware that there is a crisis on both fronts. Especially in times such as these, when we face a breakdown of established understandings and ways, self-serving pragmatic needs tend to replace a vision of an ideal social order. Instead of working diligently in the world to shape an alternative future, we allow pragmatic, rational, efficient, task-oriented survival concerns to restrain the vision and all energy is channeled toward carefully controlled institutional objectives. Institutionalism—not the same thing as accepting institutional elements or visible structures in the church—turns proper means into idolatrous ends.

A healthy church maintains a tension between the polarities of form and reform, pragmatism and vision. A healthy society and a healthy church require a dynamic tension between conservatives who work responsibly to maintain the truth of the old order and progressives who work responsibly to shape a new order. The universal ideal of humaneness based upon a future vision of God's reign to come must be held in tension with the reality of a new humanity already established through the action of God in Jesus Christ.

In Christ, the royal messiah and the suffering prophet are united. Christ pointed to a vision of the world redeemed, sanctified, and made whole—a new world that has already come, is coming even now, and is yet to come. The church as the body of Christ must embody the royal messiah and suffering prophet and must maintain the tension of form and reform, pragmatism and vision, ever aware that God does not act in a timeless heavenly drama but in the context of world affairs, with the material of unclear choices, within the reality of tainted structures.

It is important that we accept the responsibility of striving to integrate our vision into the pragmatic realities of this world. We live in the now and not yet, between the times. Now the church embodies the rule of God, but not yet does it fulfill its role in faithfulness. We pray that we may become who we are already in Christ, a new humanity. We pray that the world may become what it is intended to be, a community of peace and justice.

We commit ourselves to the task of reform, knowing that the God who becomes incarnate and acts in this world takes seriously its political and economic and social structures, but that our labor is necessarily conditioned by the limited possibilities of all worldly structures. We work at reform with no illusions of success but in grateful response to divine grace. We accept the power of weakness and the weakness of power, pragmatic visionaries living in tension between form and reform.

To be a Christian is to participate actively in a community of faith, the church. We need the church because as humans we were created to need the support of others. We need to resist the pressures to conform to the dehumanizing aspects of contemporary life or act for the transformation of society, but we cannot do this alone or just as members of a family.

We need the church because we cannot, by ourselves or within our families, satisfactorily deal with all our joys and sorrows, hopes and fears, faith and doubts, loves and hates. We need a larger community with which to share our tragedies and which can minister to us in our times of need.

We need the church to help us discern God's will for our lives. No person or family alone can adequately test the spirits or make faithful decisions amidst the ever-changing and new moral situations confronting us. Further, we need the church to correct us when we have been unfaithful and to forgive us, so that we might mature in our relationship to God, self, neighbor, and natural world.

If the church is to fulfill these responsibilities, it will need to become a mid-community or base community between the primary groups—the families or households—in which people live and the secondary social institutions in which they work. Such a base community, while not identical to a family, is more like a family than a social institution.

Luther, in his Large Catechism, differentiated between *Gemeinschaft* and *Gesellschaft*, between primary and secondary community; he contended that the church, if it was to be the church, had to be more like the first than the second. Unfortunately, over time the opposite has occurred; the church has become more institutional and less familial.

Increasingly, people are looking for a base community to help them live more meaningfully and humanely in their families or household units as well as in social institutions. The church can, and I believe must, become just such a community. Its mission and ministry are dependent upon its doing so.

Both families and social institutions (1) have a proper focus for their life, (2) have roles and responsibilities for their members, (3) demonstrate appropriate ways for members to relate to each other, (4) establish a manner of ordering life, (5) make legitimate claims on their members, and (6) have means for judging the worth of each person in the community. Let us examine each of these.

1. *Focus.* While institutions tend to focus on some particular societal concern such as health care, manufacturing of goods, banking, or education, a family maintains within its purview a concern for every aspect of life. Families deal with life in general while institutions tend to specialize. A high degree of specialization is a characteristic of the modern age, but families cannot specialize and survive.

There is surfacing once again a tendency for the church to become an institution which specializes in religion. Some church leaders in denominations that have demonstrated a concern for the economic, political, and social dimensions of life are retreating to a concern for religion. While one could argue that this shift is necessary because the religious has been neglected, the rhetoric suggests that these leaders are forgetting these other dimensions and concentrating on the religious so as to keep and attract members.

On the other hand, when the church does speak out and become involved in the political, economic, and social dimensions of life, persons in these realms suggest that the church is overstepping its bounds and should go back to worrying about the religious domain, leaving these other areas to the specialists.

If the church is essentially a social institution, it may choose to place its sole attention on the religious domain. But if the church is to be a community of faith, a base community more like a family than an institution, then it must be concerned about every aspect of human life and seek to integrate the religious, social, political, and economic on behalf of justice and fullness of human life for all people.

2. *Responsibilities.* We share only a piece of ourselves with the institutions within which we work and the voluntary associations to which we belong. Within these social institutions we assume particular, identifiable responsibilities. I may be a truck driver, nurse, computer programmer, lawyer, bank teller, or store owner; I may be an organization president, secretary, chairperson, or committee member. In each case we are clear about our responsibilities and involve ourselves accordingly. But life in a family is different. We may assume assigned responsibilities, but the family has a claim on all our time and energy, it makes rightful demands on our total personality. It expects a total commitment and some involvement in every aspect of its life.

Within the institutional church we limit our involvement to assigned responsibilities. We are lectors, catechists, board members, and so forth. But in a community of faith, while we necessarily assume responsibilities and move in and out of roles as needed, we are expected to be completely committed and involved in the total life of that community.

3. *Depth of Relationships.* Institutional life makes few emotional demands. Relationships within institutions are goal- and task-oriented. We are expected to keep our emotions to ourselves and behave effectively and efficiently. Acts of caring for one another's needs are limited and extracurricular. Most of us have experienced the dis-ease if someone breaks down in the middle of a meeting and cries. We are concerned, but our feelings appear inappropriate. Why couldn't the person have waited until we had finished our task? But families are different. The depth of relationships within a family both necessitates and encourages honest sharing of emotions and concern for each person's condition.

In an institutional church human needs are met by someone assigned that responsibility; but in a community of faith activities can be put aside so that the whole community can respond to individual needs and thereby demonstrate the depth of relationship that is integral to community life.

A beautiful example of this reality in process occurred once when I was giving an address to a large group of church persons. In the middle of the address someone suffered a seizure. The leader whispered for me to stop, told the group that the person was being helped, and said, "Sing with me." In a moment the whole group was quietly singing a prayer for calm, healing, peace, and love. "Let us offer a prayer of thanksgiving," she said, as the person with the seizure left the room. Then she whispered to me, "Go on; now you can pick up where we left off."

4. *Ordering of Life.* Institutions have explicit rules, regulations, constitutions, and bylaws that regulate how each person is to behave and how business is to be conducted. In a family, however, life is regulated by customs, that is, implicitly. Everyone is expected to know how family members are to behave. They may choose to do otherwise, but if the family is healthy, they know what responsible family life looks like.

When our own children were young, they would often appeal to my wife and me by saying, "But everyone is doing it." Our response would be, "That is very fine, but that is not the Westerhoff way." And when they were older and would go out for the evening, we would say, "Have a good time, but remember that you are a Westerhoff." Our appeal was to who we were, to our identity as a family, and to the character of life shared and learned through communal living over the years.

The church as an institution needs laws and regulations to order its life; when members want to know how to conduct corporate life, they should be able to appeal to constitutions and bylaws. However, by shared experience and role models the church as an intimate community of faith establishes an implicit awareness of the norms and principles for life. A community of faith has a character that makes possible the ordering of life by custom and requires only an appeal to identity to show persons how they are to live. Instead of complex lists of laws for moral behavior, a community of faith equips its people to ask, As a believer of Jesus Christ and a member of his church what am I to do?

5. *Obligations.* Within institutions obligations are limited. They are established by contracts which clearly state what each party is to do and therefore can anticipate from the other. If the contract is broken by one party, the other is no longer obligated to keep it. In a family, however, obligations are founded on whatever love demands. There are persons today who would like

to make marriage a contract, but I am convinced that to do so would mean the demise of the family. Within the new Episcopal marriage rite a great deal of freedom for creativity is permitted, but no couple can write their own marriage vows. If the couple is unwilling to make the vows established by the church, the church cannot bless the marriage. And those vows are clear: They are a promise to love unconditionally forever.

Members of the institutional church make what amounts to contracts. If the church fulfills what it is expected to say and do, then the member is loyal and supportive; but if the church does not, then the member leaves or withdraws support. In a community of faith persons promise to love unconditionally and give to the community whatever love demands.

I recall, for example, a man who was very much opposed to the new Episcopal *Book of Common Prayer.* He did everything within his power to oppose its adoption. There were others who shared his convictions. When the new prayer book was adopted, two opponents stopped attending worship and withdrew their financial pledges. This man, on the other hand, continued to attend and, when he discovered what his friends had done, increased his own gift to compensate for theirs as well. "I'll never like or approve of this new prayer book," he said one day, "but the church is family."

6. *Evaluating Worth.* Within institutions a person's worth is judged by performance and evaluated by contribution. The greater the contribution and the more valuable the performance, the greater the person's worth. On the basis of performance people are rewarded and affirmed. But in a family, at its best, worth is based simply on being. Every family has at least one "crazy" or irresponsible Uncle Harry or Aunt Jane, but these persons are accepted as they are. In the institutional church people are evaluated and affirmed according to their contributions and rewarded according to

their acceptability; in a community of faith everyone is accepted no matter how unacceptable, persons are loved though unlovable. Each person is seen as a child of God, a sheep of Christ's fold, a sinner of Christ's redeeming, ever in the image of God, no matter how distorted. All persons are of worth simply because they bear the mark of the crucified one who died that they might know that in God's eyes each one is worth everything and always worthy.

In our world, where justice is supposed to be dispassionate and unbiased, where we are to be rewarded and punished according to our deserving, a Christian community of faith is called to an alternative way of seeing life and an alternative identity. We are called to be a community that displays a biased passion for the outsider, the stranger, and the estranged and gives people what they need, not what they deserve.

7

Christian Nurture in a Faith Community

Christian nurture is a contemporary expression for the historic word "catechesis." Catechesis, or Christian nurture, both assumes and indeed is dependent upon experience and reflection within a faith community. Catechesis assumes a communal understanding of human nature and the necessity of a faithful community: a community that shares a common memory and vision, a community conscious of its roots and committed to its vision of the future, a community with a common authority, a community with common rituals or repetitive symbolic actions expressing its memory and vision, and a community that in its common life is more like a family than a social institution or voluntary association.

Christian nurture or catechesis also has the following characteristics:

1. Catechesis is comprised of two interrelated processes: formation and education. Formation takes seriously what we know about enculturation or socialization. It is an intentional, relational-experiential activity within the life of a faith community that, for example, shapes perceptions or faith, shapes consciousness, and shapes character.

Education takes seriously what we know about teaching and learning. It is an intentional activity that aids in acquiring those behaviors—thinking (intellectual and intuitive), feeling, and willing—needed for responsible life in the church and world. And education also takes seriously what we know about *praxis*, prophetic judgment or critical reflection on experience and action. It is an intentional critical-reflective activity within a community of faith that stimulates within persons a critical dialogue between their life experience and the tradition.

Catechesis as formation inducts persons into the church and its story. Catechesis as education aids persons in making the community's faith more living, conscious, and active in their lives.

Through formational processes, a person acquires and sustains the tradition. Such processes aim to conserve and to provide roots in the past. As such, they are intentional, experiential, socializing, nurturing processes within every aspect of parish life. Further, they are fundamental to the whole catechetical process.

Through educational processes a person critically examines the tradition, reshapes it when necessary, accepts it, and applies it to life. Such processes aim to transform and to provide openness to the future. As such, they are intentional, reflective, understanding, reforming processes related to every aspect of parish life. They are secondary to the formational processes; in both sequence and cognitive development they necessarily follow experience.

There is also a third important aspect of catechesis: an integrative reflective task that helps to relate life in the church and life in the world. For example, spiritual life includes both an interior experience, the direct encounter with God resulting in a personal knowledge of God, *and* exterior manifestation, daily life lived in an ever-deepening love relationship to God and, therefore, to neighbor. Catechesis helps persons to reflect on prayer as exterior manifestation and to prepare for meaningful prayer as interior experience, as well as to reflect on this interior experience as preparation for faithful life in the world.

2. Catechesis always includes both converting and nurturing dimensions. It is concerned with a conserving need to form persons in the tradition of the church and a transforming need to liberate persons from erroneous understandings and ways of life and to reform church belief and practice. Catechesis—an adult activity as much as one for children or youth—implies a dialogue between the tradition and life experience.

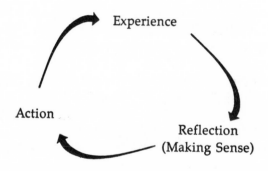

Experience

Action

Reflection
(Making Sense)

3. The processes of catechesis are understood best in terms of a circle of experience, reflection, and action. Typically we act before we experience, we experience *we learn* before we make sense, and we act upon our beliefs. *experience*

4. The processes of catechesis are related to readiness rather than time, to appropriateness rather than packaged formats. The key is readiness, not the completion of a particular course of study. Different persons have different learning needs, learning styles, and capacities for learning. We must tailor catechesis to handle the great diversity in human need and potential, rather than try to fit persons into established programs and organizations.

This human diversity is reflected in Greek mythology. Zeus commissions four gods to make humans

complete: Apollo, Dionysus, Prometheus, and Epime-
theus. Hippocrates wrote of four temperaments in human beings—sanguine, choleric, phlegmatic, and mel-
ancholic—which the German psychiatrist Kretschmer
translated into four psychological temperaments. C. G.
Jung described four personality types: sensate-think-
ing, sensate-feeling, intuitive-thinking, and intuitive-
feeling; when combined with his two other functions,
these make for a typology of sixteen personalities.
Urban Holmes describes four historic schools of spiritu-
ality: speculative-kataphatic, affective-kataphatic, affec-
tive-apophatic, and speculative-apophatic. Modern
learning theory speaks of four types of learners and
management theory of four leadership types.

While each of these theories is unique, there is a
fascinating and amazing overlap between them. Of
course, these are all typologies and not intended to be
closed structures in which to place oneself or others.
Each type is understood to be of value and all are necessary for wholeness. No one person is a pure type; but in
most people the characteristics of one or two types are
predominant, and most people prefer to function as one
or two of the types.

These various typologies can be integrated into what
I will call alpha, beta, gamma, and delta personalities.
It should be obvious that each person encompasses all of
these functions. While in any one person one or two of
these functions may be dominant, a healthy community
must show an integration and balance of all four. In
terms of these four personality types, it is possible to
characterize their typical, preferred ways of being in the
world, ways of relating to God, ways of learning, and
ways of behaving in a group.

Alpha Persons. Typically these persons rely for
knowledge on their senses. They tend to care most
about the present, the external meaning of events, and
continuity with the past. They are logical, systematic,

highly rational people who enjoy speculation but insist on objective analysis and principled decision making. In a parish you will typically find them seeking out study groups and pushing for better sermons.

Spiritually they are most concerned about the illumination of the mind through imaginal techniques. Mental prayer leading to discernment is natural for such persons, and exercises such as the Ignatian examination of consciousness are considered helpful.

Such persons tend to be bright in terms of facts and always seek the "right" answer. They learn best in formal, structured environments using textbooks and lectures; they need an expert teacher. Their involvement in the world is aimed at influencing thought, and in a group they are typically negotiators and problem solvers. They have a tendency, however, toward dogmatism. They tend to be highly critical of others and show an excessive concern for reason and right thinking.

Beta Persons. Typically these persons also rely on their senses for knowledge and care most about the present, the external meaning of events, and continuity with the past. However, they make their decisions on the basis of a personal value system and subjective criteria. Typically they are idealists rather than realists, who in a parish seek small, caring groups and desire more emotion and intimacy in worship.

Spiritually they are most concerned about the illumination of the heart through imaginal techniques. Meditative prayer leading to the experience of presence is natural for beta persons, and exercises such as the Way of the Cross are helpful. Charismatics in this group will desire emotive worship while others will find communal offices sung daily more to their liking.

These folk seem only to learn from experience and in small groups when they are sensually and affectively involved. They require a loving teacher who is a companion and friend. Their involvement in the world is aimed at influencing people's attitudes, and in a group they are typically stabilizers and consolidators. As such, they are more interested in the process than the product. They have a tendency, however, toward pietism. They tend to be extremely sentimental and show an excessive concern for emotions and right experiences.

Gamma Persons. Typically these persons rely on their imaginations for knowledge. They tend to care most about the future, the internal meaning of events, and change. While they are intuitive visionaries, they still insist on logical, systematic, objective analysis and enjoy speculation. In a parish you will find them in groups concerned for social involvement and action. They seek to make worship more related to daily life, and they want their parish to be an example in society.

Spiritually they are concerned with the illumination of the head, but through emptying techniques that are aimed at "direct" intuitive insight. Active prayer leading to witness is natural for gamma persons, and techniques such as bringing the petitions of the Lord's Prayer before God as questions ("How can your kingdom come through me this day?"), intuiting God's response, requesting that gift, and going forth to use it are helpful.

These persons are naturally curious and filled with why questions. They learn best in laboratory settings or through projects. They enjoy inventing and testing theories. They are independent, serious learners for whom work is play. While they learn by involved experimentation, they need a directing teacher.

Their involvement in the world is aimed at influencing behavior and in a group they are typically conceptualizers and designers of action. They tend to be highly committed, serious folk who have a tendency toward moralism, demonstrate an excessive concern for right actions, and sometimes express a desire to separate themselves from the culture.

Delta Persons. Typically these persons also rely on their imaginations for knowledge. They care most about the future, the internal meaning of events, and change. They are intuitive visionaries. However, they make their decisions on the basis of a personal value system and subjective criteria. For the most part they are idealists. In a parish they are most concerned about their relationship with the divine through solitude and silence. They desire retreats and space for prayer and devotion.

Spiritually they are most concerned with the illumination of the heart through emptying techniques. Contemplative prayer leading to mystical union with God is natural for delta persons, and exercises such as the Jesus prayer or breath prayer are helpful. They learn best by creative expression through the arts. They are daydreamers who live in their imaginations and are always seeking to create something new. They learn by observation and therefore need a teacher who can be a role model.

Their involvement in the world is aimed at offering people an alternative, and in a group they are catalysts and enablers. They have a tendency, however, to quietism or an excessive concern for union with God that moves them toward a contemplative life and away from the world, with a resultant neglect of the culture.

Another aspect of human life that catechesis takes seriously is the personal and social conditions of people at particular points in their life histories. The most obvious is age and its related physiological, psychosocial, mental, and religious stages of development. Children of ten are typically not able to think, relate, believe, or act in ways possible for twenty-year-olds. Similarly, forty-year-olds face unique problems and special needs that limit what they can do, as well as influence what issues they need to address before they can do anything else.

Persons also have particular underdeveloped and developed talents and skills that confront them with both limitations and obligations. For example, if a person has a talent for writing but no talent for being a politician, it would be unwise for that person to seek public office and neglect to develop and use the skill of writing to influence political life.

Some persons are poor and others wealthy, some are sick and others healthy, some possess great power and influence and others little, some have a great deal of leisure time and others none. Each of these personal and social conditions, conditions that may change over time, both limit and oblige individuals to particular behaviors and responsibilities. The church must not encourage persons to do what they cannot do or make them feel guilty for not doing so. However, the church needs to encourage, stimulate, and equip persons to do all that they can do.

If we have a communal attitude toward life we can accept the fact that no one can do everything—or needs to try. But we must believe that whatever we do will make a significant difference. Each of us must be honest about ourselves, continue to grow and develop our gifts and graces, increase our commitment to God's reign, and be faithful in doing all that we can where we live and work in the firm belief that this is all God requires of us.

5. The end of catechesis is a lifestyle which includes our total being as thinking, feeling, willing persons. It is not solely a concern for believing certain doctrines (whether understood or not), having particular religious experiences, or a willingness to be a part of a particular denomination. A Christian lifestyle includes *character*, a sense of who we are and of the dispositions, attitudes, and values related to that identity; *conscience*,

an activity of the whole person making rational decisions, as a believer in Jesus Christ and as a member of his church, about what is a faithful act; and conduct, a life that others see as a sign of and witness to the sovereignty of God.

6. Catechesis is a personal pilgrimage with companions in community. It is not a process of molding individuals into some predetermined design or of simply aiding individuals to grow up according to some pattern. That is, it is not doing things to or for persons. It is, rather, a process of journeying with others within a community; sharing life together over some route of travel, acting and reflecting with others. It assumes searchers, persons who are willing to let *their* lives be a resource for others and who are convinced that truth is revealed to all as they share in this mutual quest.

Our spiritual pilgrimage can best be understood in terms of three pathways to God. Each trail leads to God, so none is superior to the others. While the first path is a natural place to begin and therefore appears appropriate for children, each path may be traveled at any time. On a pilgrimage the process of traveling is as important as the end of the trip; so it is beneficial to travel each route. Indeed, we miss something if we limit ourselves to one trail, yet all these pathways reach the same goal or summit.

The first path I have named the *Experiential Way*. On this slow, easy path the community focuses its efforts on the transmission and acquisition of its story (its memory and vision). Dealing with perceiving and knowing, it aids in the necessary formation of our individual and corporate identity as a story-formed people.

In community, persons are helped to participate in a family-like, caring, nurturing fellowship. Subjective experience is central, while religious conversions expressed in terms of a falling in love with God are necessary. Together persons seek after intuitive knowledge that is nurtured through participation in the arts and expressed through symbols, myths, and rituals.

The authority of the community is assumed and trusted in the necessary conserving task of establishing a tradition. The aim on this first path is to establish a personal identity as a child of God who lives in a dependent relationship with God and as a communal being dependent on others for guidance and help in learning to live as a pilgrim.

The second path I have named the *Reflective Way*. This is a difficult and sometimes painful traversing of rocks. The community encourages persons to be vulnerable in the search for meaning and purpose by striving to make sense of their lives in the light of the community's story. Dealing with believing and understanding, this path aids in the necessary process of individuation and growing into trustful intimacy with others.

In community, persons are encouraged to assume responsibility for their own faith and lives. Objective reflection is central, while intellectual conversions expressed in terms of commitment are necessary. Together persons quest after intellectual knowledge nurtured by critical reflection on their experience and expressed in signs, concepts, and moral actions.

The authority of the community is tested by the learned ability to integrate Scripture-tradition, reason, and experience as all seek to reshape the tradition and live prophetically in society. As they journey along together in absolute dependence upon God, persons are helped to establish a sense of autonomy in their relationships with each other.

The third path I have named the *Integrating Way*. On this path the community encourages persons to resolve any dissonance that may have been experienced by traversing the other two ways. Dealing with discerning and willing, this way helps persons to address the questions, How am I as a believer in Jesus Christ and a member of his story-formed community to act? How can I best live in community for the benefit of others? Moral conversions of commitment, which aid persons to choose freely and to will God's will, are necessary.

Together persons combine intuitive and intellectual ways of knowing and find meaning in both contemplation and action. They see the world as having two dimensions, the spiritual and the material, the sacred and the secular. On this path the community seeks to reconcile the paradox of catholic substance and its need to conserve the tradition with a reformed spirit of prophetic judgment and retraditioning.

Persons are no longer caught between either believing that there is *the* truth that their authority knows and that must be blindly accepted, and/or believing that there is no truth and everyone is his or her own authority. Now they are able to deal with pluralism's options without becoming relativistic. They accept truth for their own lives and advocate this truth, yet they are able to remain open to others. Within community, still radically and totally dependent upon God, they seek to live in interdependent relationship with each other as an apostolic witness in society. In the words of T. S. Eliot: "We shall not cease from exploration and the end of all our exploring will be to arrive where we started and know the place for the first time" (from "Little Gidding" from *Four Quartets*, in *The Norton Anthology of English Literature*, ed. M. H. Abrams [New York: Norton, 1968] 2:2197).

Those on this third path are able to affirm and aid those traveling on the other two ways, but also have persons on the other two paths to help them maintain their integrative way. Persons on the first path keep those on the second from going too far afield and help them move to the integrative trail. Those on the second path help those on the first to move toward a new way. And so it goes, each person in need of the others, each contributing to the life of the others. A healthy community of faith has persons on all three paths and encourages all of them on their journeys.

7. Catechesis particularly relates to the liturgical life of the church. First, catechesis is necessary to introduce persons to the church's rituals.

Second, catechesis takes place covertly within the ritual itself. So symbolic actions need reform to insure that they point to the reality intended.

Third, catechesis takes place overtly in the liturgy of the Word, or what was known as the rite of the catechumens. If we took learning seriously, this part of the ritual could be more effective. For example, we would never read to a friend part of a letter from another friend in the manner we typically read Paul's letters in worship. And much of the Hebrew Scripture was originally folk music. It might better be remembered if it were set to music and sung. We could also retell stories as stories and dramatize the drama of the Scripture.

Fourth, catechesis is necessary to help people reflect on their daily lives as they prepare for participation in the ritual; catechesis is also necessary to help people reflect on the ritual as they prepare for daily life. Unless we prepare people for reflection that strives to relate cultural and daily life, our celebrating of the Eucharist will lack vitality and authenticity, and our living of the Eucharist will lack significant power and witness. With the aid of catechesis before and after worship, the integration of celebrating and living the Eucharist can be achieved with greater faithfulness.

If we understand these characteristics of catechesis, further implications should be obvious. We need to examine our common life and become more critical of every aspect of parish life. We need to discover to what degree our life is an expression of culture and to what degree it is faithful to the gospel. We need to contemplate whether we have interpreted the gospel through a cultural perceptual field or whether the gospel is providing us with the perceptual field necessary to transform our culture. Both experience and reflection must be taken seriously.

In order for catechesis to be faithful, the church must be striving to become a moral community of mature Christians providing a context in which to experience and reflect upon the gospel for themselves and those they adopt into the family, whether adults or infants. That is, the church must be an ever-reforming, nurturing, caring community of faith and life.

Catechesis addresses the nature and character of these interactive, dialectical processes by which persons mature in the faith of the church as they live into their baptism. Catechesis is sharing in a lifelong pilgrimage of daily conversions and nurture within a story-formed, sacramental community. Catechesis is being ever shaped by the gospel tradition within a community that moves from experience to reflection to action day by day throughout a person's lifetime.

Thus, catechesis addresses the ends and means of believing, being, and behaving in community. In catechesis deliberate, systematic, and sustained interpersonal helping relationships of acknowledged value aid persons within a faith community to know God, to live in relationship to God, and to act with God in the world.

Catechesis attempts to provide persons with a communal context for living into their baptism, an environment for experiencing the ever converting and nurturing presence of Christ as they gather day by day in community in the Lord's name to be confronted with God's Word, respond to the gift of faith, pray for the world and the church, share God's peace, present the offerings of their lives and labor, give thanksgiving for

God's grace, break bread and share the gift of God, and are thereby nourished to love and serve the Lord that they might be a sign of God's kingdom come.

Catechesis attempts to provide persons with a context for falling in love with Christ, having their eyes and ears opened to perceive and experience personally the gospel of God's kingdom, living in a growing relationship with Christ, and reflecting and acting with Christ on behalf of God's coming kingdom.

We humans are communal beings; we cannot be human alone. Liturgy is the activity of persons in community. All constructions of reality are social constructions; none are the result solely of individual experience or of individual logical, rational analysis. The construction of religious meaning is a social construction and is impossible outside community. Authority both proceeds from communal life and is essential for communal life. Authority for all ultimate convictions is in the end dependent upon community.

Truth is process as well as proposition. Truth is both the meaning of life and the process of making sense of experience within a story-formed sacramental community. Authority is what possesses the power to explain and justify, inspire, and judge this process of making sense and establishing meaning. Authority includes the intuitive and intellectual activities of a community whose life is shaped by a particular story and vision.

To be sure, Christianity is a "revealed religion," revealed in the sense that it proceeds from particular communal experiences and results in knowledge that we could not attain on our own or by any rational process alone. Christian faith makes the radical claim that Jesus Christ is the sacrament of God, both the truth and the authority for the truth.

The Fourth Evangelist records Jesus as saying, "I am the way, the truth, and the life" (John 14:6), that is,

"Through my life the mystery of life's meaning is revealed." In Jesus, the manifestation of God, truth is
unveiled or made present. How are we to know that
truth? The Fourth Gospel answers, "Live by the truth"
(John 3:21, Jerusalem Bible), that is, *Do it.*" But what
does it mean to do the truth? It means to participate in
Christ's being, his body the church. "Participation in
my life will aid you in making sense of your life, indeed
of all life."

Those of us who have been socialized in North
America tend to interpret Christianity from either an
individual or an organizational perspective. Yet Christian truth makes no sense outside of community. Baptism is neither a response to a call for individual salvation nor the joining of an organization; it is
incorporation into a community.

The priest Vincent Donavan in *Christianity Rediscovered*, his epistle from the Masai, shares how after a
year of evangelization among the Masai he met with the
old man who headed the community. Father Donavan
proceeded to sort out for the elderly gentleman those
who rarely attended church, those who didn't understand the faith, and those whose lives had shown no
noticeable change because of it. "Padri," the old man
stopped him politely but firmly, "why are you trying to
break us up and separate us? During the year you have
visited us, we have talked around the fire after you
departed. Of course, there have been the lazy ones, but
they have been helped by those with much energy.
There have been the stupid ones, but they have been
helped by the intelligent. There have been ones of little
faith, but they have been helped by those with much
faith. From the first day you came, I have spoken for
these people, and I speak for them now. We have
reached the place where we can say, 'We believe.'"

"We believe—communal faith," pondered Father
Donavan. Then he recalled the old rite for the baptism

-99-

of infants. "What do you ask of the church?" he would inquire of the child. Of course, the infant couldn't answer, but the infant's sponsors would supply the response "Faith." Donavan reflects, "We come to the church not because we have faith but because we desire faith and know that it can only be ours if we live in a community of faith."

He looked at the old man, "Excuse me, old man, sometimes my head is hard and learns slowly. 'We believe,' you said; of course you do. Everyone in the community will be baptized."

Christians are made, not born. By baptism we are made Christians. However, we often miss the radical nature of this symbolic action. In the case of children, godparents, who represent the "faith family" and act as sponsors for the child, bring the child before the community so that the child might be drowned (killed) and reborn and thereby begin life afresh, outside the bounds of biological kinship. The child is given up by its parents for adoption into a new family and acquires both a personal baptismal name and a new faith-family surname—Christian. The child is then signed (branded) with a cross so that the child and the world will always know to whom she or he belongs. The child's new brothers and sisters accept him or her into the family, make a covenant to assume responsibility for their life together, greet the child with a holy kiss, and then share a meal together at their faith-family dinner table. The same action occurs with adults, except that they make a conscious decision to engage in this radical action.

Under the rubrics of the 1979 *Book of Common Prayer*, parishes of the Episcopal Church in the United States celebrate baptisms five times each year at a community Eucharist. Those five times, chosen for catechetical purposes, are the Easter Vigil, Pentecost, All Saints' Day, Jesus' Baptism (Sunday after the Epiphany), and the

-100-

visitation of the bishop. These occasions can help the church understand its vocation and provide opportunity for its members to review their lives and renew their baptismal covenants as they progress in community on the human, vocational pilgrimage of living into their baptism.

At Easter we are reminded that we have been killed and born again in the image of God. At Pentecost we are reminded that we have been reunited with the Spirit of God and can live fully as that Spirit expresses its gifts in our common lives. At All Saints' Day we are reminded that we are now saints, perfect people, royalty, and that all we need do is to acknowledge our true human condition and be who we really are. At Jesus' Baptism we are reminded that our vocation is to be manifested in ministry with Christ, with our life in the world, a sign and a witness to the transformation of all human life and the reign of God. And last, at the visitation of the bishop we are reminded that we have been adopted into a new family, God's family, so that we might have life and have it abundantly, living in love for all persons and in obedience to the will of God.

Through preparatory catechesis and the repetition of the baptismal renewal ritual we are provided with an opportunity to reform our lives continually as persons living in a faith family and to so be granted the gift of community necessary for the humanizing of life. The questions asked in the Episcopal *Book of Common Prayer* are these:

Do you reaffirm your renunciation of evil? At baptism a person turns away from and therefore negates the power of three kinds of evil: cosmic evil, those spiritual forces that rebel against God (for example, natural tragedies); social evil, those institutions and systems we humans create that disrupt and destroy persons (for example, war, systemic racism, and sexism); and personal evil, those sinful desires which draw us from the love of God and neighbor (for example, greed, lust, pride, and avarice).

Do you renew your commitment to Jesus Christ? In the baptismal liturgy we announce our turning away from evil and our turning to Jesus Christ, who saves us from the evil one and thereby makes it possible for us to be whole and holy. We further announce that we are putting our trust in his grace, his unmerited love, as the means by which we can actualize our new life. And last, we promise to follow and obey him, to live a life that is a sign and a witness to that gift of love. We need continually to reflect on our lives and examine who or what has power over us and is claiming our loyalty. We need to explore the perceptions that inform our lives by reviewing our understanding of the Christian story. That story is our corporate memory of how God has been active in the history of the world and of our people in the past and present. And it is our understanding of the Christian vision, our picture of the reign of God, where love triumphs over hate, hope over despair, and life over death.

The Apostles' Creed. The next element in the renewal of our baptismal covenant is a reaffirmation of the Apostles' Creed, those convictions of the heart to which we give our loyalty, namely, one God known as creator, redeemer, and perfecter or sanctifier. We need to explore imaginatively and rationally the meanings behind this love song and its implications for individual and corporate life.

First, we need to reflect on what it means to say that God is creator and that we are made in God's image. At least normatively, this conviction implies an affirmation and preservation of life, no matter how deformed. If we can affirm such a view, what does it mean for us to help each other sustain humane life and be creative people?

on
about

did & st die for that life in you?
Then what right have you to kill it?

Second, what does it mean to say that God is our redeemer? Since Christ died for all, every person is of ultimate value, even the least among us. Since this affirmation calls us to give ourselves and affirm others as Christ did, we need to examine where racism, sexism, classism, nationalism, or denominationalism are present in our individual and corporate lives.

Third, we need to reflect on what it means to say God is our perfecter or sanctifier, the one who makes life whole and holy. Minimally it affirms that the essential nature of life is in relationship with self, God, neighbor, and the natural world, just as it deplores anything that divides or distorts personal or communal life.

Having reflected on the creed, its meanings, and implications, we are ready to turn to the specific promises related to living out our baptismal covenant:

Will you continue in the apostles' teaching and fellowship, in the breaking of bread, and in the prayers? Behind this promise is a commitment to the rational study of Holy Scripture, to shared life in an historic faith community, to participation in the Eucharist and the other liturgical aspects of church life, and to a disciplined spiritual life.

Will you persevere in resisting evil, and, whenever you fall into sin, repent and return to the Lord? Here is an opportunity to consider and participate in the rite of reconciliation; it is also a time to reflect on how we might best resist social and personal evil and engage in catechesis to encourage, sustain, and support such behavior. It is a time we reflect on the seven deadly dispositions to sin and the practice of the virtues, a time we contemplate what evil needs to be resisted and how we might support each other in that resistance.

Will you proclaim by word and example the Good News of God in Christ? Here is an opportunity to reflect on the needs of those for whom the Good News is announced: the hurt, the captive, the oppressed, the sick, the hungry, the needy, the lost, the troubled, all those denied the benefits of life in God's redeemed world, those who know only the bad news of the evening news. It is a time to reflect on "acts-evangelism," the means by which we can act to bring good news and then tell the story of Jesus if we are asked why we act as we do. It means asking how we can be a sign of God's reign in the lives of all people and make an evangelical witness to God's kingdom come. It is also a time for us to reflect on the Good News as it speaks to our lives and to share our experience of the redeeming love of God.

Will you seek to serve Christ in all persons, loving your neighbor as yourself? Here is an opportunity to reflect on the meaning of ministry in church and society, to strive to discern the ministry to which God is calling us at this point in our lives, and to prepare ourselves for engaging in that ministry.

Will you strive for justice and peace among all people and respect the dignity of every human being? Here is an opportunity to reflect on our personal and corporate action on behalf of the gospel. Most persons in the church can understand acts of Christian service to the needy, but they have difficulty understanding social, political, and economic action that is intended to make our acts of mercy unnecessary. This is also a time to reflect on how we indirectly or directly support actions in our community, church, nation, state, or place of employment that work against liberation and justice, reconciliation and peace. More important, it is a time to decide what we can do through nonviolent resistance to change those social structures that prevent God's shalom.

By continually renewing our baptismal covenant we live into our baptism, we become who we already are. This pilgrimage necessarily takes place within a faith family. Accurately describing this pilgrimage, a Lutheran pastor tells of visiting a parish in Texas near the Mexican border. When he arrived, he was told that a

Mexican child named Israel would be baptized. Wishing to give Israel a gift, my friend went shopping across the border and fell in love with a pair of sandals suitable for a ten-year-old. When he told the shopkeeper of his problem, she replied, "Don't worry; he can grow into them." He bought the sandals and told his story to Israel's parents, who understood the symbolism of the sandals: baptism is a walk, a way of life. *a walk we learn — as shoes walk sandals new*

Six months later the pastor returned and learned that Israel's cousin Lisa was to be baptized. He went to look for another present. This time he fell in love with booties for a child of two months. But Lisa was ten months old. He was explaining his problem to the shopkeeper when she interrupted him and said, "Don't worry; she can hang them on the wall to remind her of her baptism." As he bought them, he became aware in a new way that baptism means going somewhere, being on the way. Baptism is living between booties and sandals, between remembering and growing into. We are all on a pilgrimage with Lisa and Israel.

To summarize: The process of catechesis or Christian nurture requires a faith community. The family, indeed all persons, require a faith community. Such a community is difficult to find, and we are often ambivalent about our desires to find one because of its demands upon us. Such a community requires commitment and effort to develop and sustain. Nevertheless, our educational ministry and all our programs and resources will be less than effective means for the transmission, maintenance, transformation, and growth of Christian faith and life unless they operate within such a community context. Consequently, if we really care about the faith, the church, the family, and Christian nurture, we will direct our attention and efforts to the characteristics of a faith community.

The church is the body of Christ, a sign of God's presence and rule in human history, a mystery even to the faithful. As such it cannot be totally understood or fully defined. The church is a community of faith, a human reality, a challenge to the human imagination and will. As such it can be described and with God's help be formed and transformed within history. And as Christian educator C. Ellis Nelson affirms, faith is communicated by a community of faith as it worships and lives in community. And the meaning of faith is developed by its people out of their common history, by their interactions with each other and in relationship to the events that take place in their lives.

We are baptized into a community of faith. How can that community aid its members on their pilgrimage of living into their baptism and fulfilling their calling to be both sign and instrument of true community—God's unfathomable union with humanity and the union of human beings among themselves? I have explored alternatives, but remain convinced that a living Christian faith demands a community of faith that shares a common story, authority, worship, and life—a community of faith engaging intentionally in those processes that best help its faith to become conscious, living, and active in the personal and corporate lives of its people.

50 "Xian faith is no leap into the absurd"

30' idea for P. L. Studen. on Xds calendar & i a preaching year (not

p2 f Mk 3:7-35 —
28 Ex 20 'honn parents
geus.

6r 27 for maybe —
B Act 2

45 II Pet 14 f

47 II Cor 3 14
86 I Jn quote, 92

104 I Jn - 'act. evaglin
105 " "aware" 9 also Eph 4 >
101-f on Xian true wories & life I Jn

5 8 f world & gosp
"Lou nees" — I J

81 14 Pereher you a love
Eph. 2, 3, 4 ?
maybe I Jn)

103 on abortion